ENCYCLOPEDIA OF INCREDIBLE THINGS

First published in 2023 by Miles Kelly Publishing Ltd
Harding's Barn, Bardfield End Green, Thaxted, Essex, CM6 3PX, UK

2 4 6 8 10 9 7 5 3 1

Publishing Director Belinda Gallagher
Creative Director Jo Cowan
Editorial Director Rosie Neave
Senior Editors Sarah Carpenter, Amy Johnson, Becky Miles
Designers Jo Cowan, Joe Jones, Venita Kidwai, Simon Lee, Emily Stalley
Indexer Becky Miles
Production Elizabeth Collins
Image Manager Liberty Newton
Reprographics Stephan Davis
Assets Venita Kidwai

ISBN 978-1-78989-821-7

Printed in China

British Library Cataloguing-in-Publication Data
A catalogue record for this book is available from the British Library

Acknowledgements
The publishers would like to thank the following artists who have contributed to this book:
Diane Ewen and Nila Aye (Animals),
Ela Smietanka and Ana Gomez (Dinosaurs),
Tony Neal and Genie Espinosa (Space),
Steven Wood and Chris Jevons (Human Body),
Elissambura (Rainforests), Paul Nicholls (Oceans)

Made with paper from a sustainable forest

www.mileskelly.net

ENCYCLOPEDIA OF INCREDIBLE THINGS

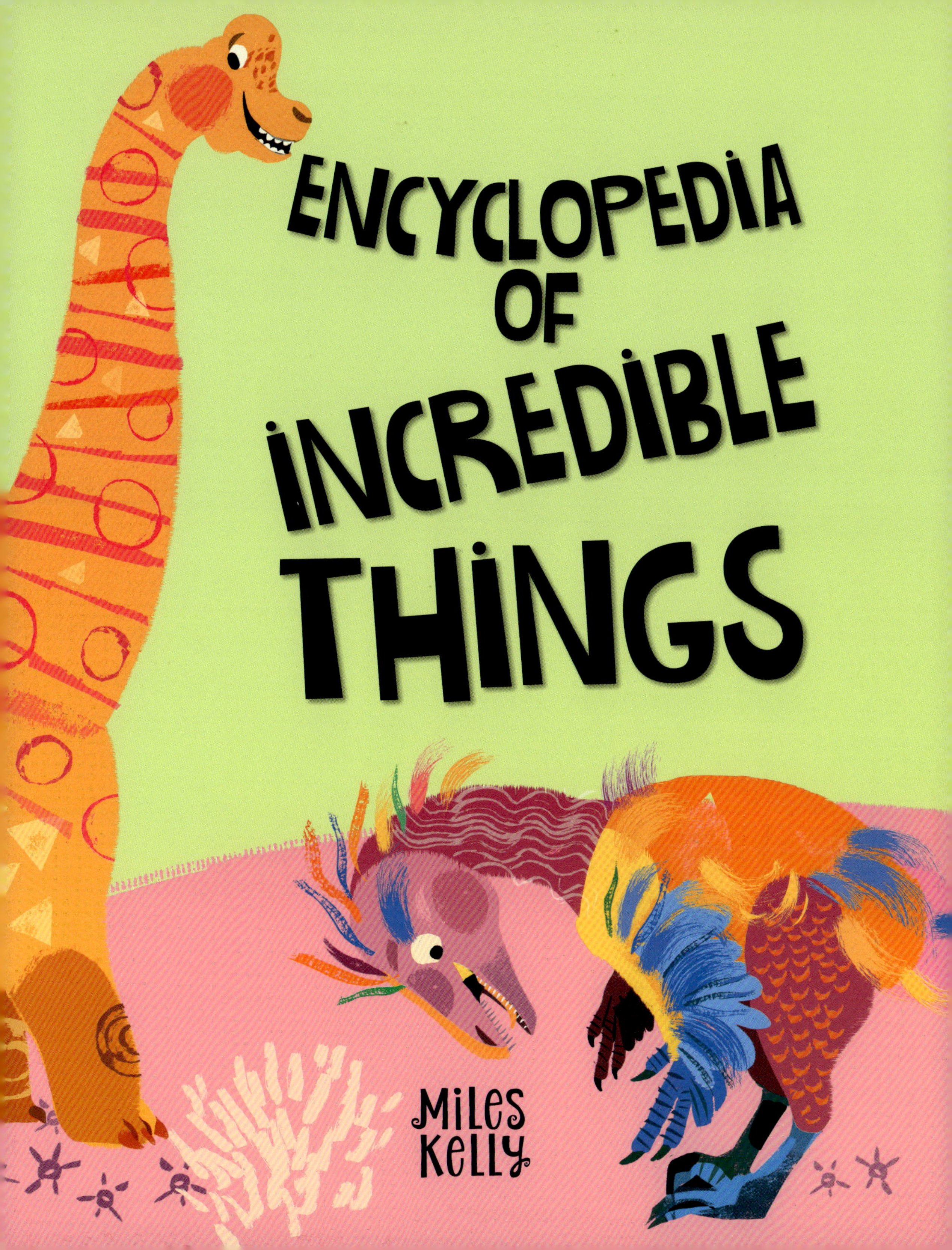

Miles Kelly

Barbara Taylor
Consultant: Anne Rooney
Clive Gifford
Consultant: Camilla de la Bédoyère
Clive Gifford
Consultant: Sue Becklake
Clive Gifford
Consultant: Kristina Routh MB ChB
Camilla de la Bédoyère
Barbara Taylor

CONTENTS

ANIMALS

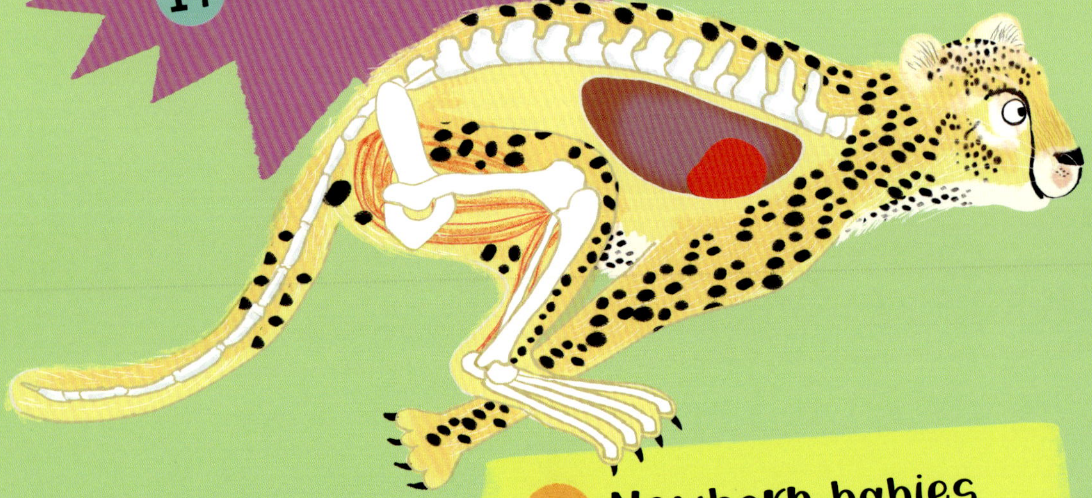

All kinds of animals

From tiny ants to enormous whales, animals come in all shapes and sizes. People are animals too! Scientists think there are nearly 8 million species (kinds) of animal on Earth.

Looking inside

Scientists divide animals into two huge groups. Animals with a backbone are called vertebrates. Animals with no backbone are called invertebrates.

Invertebrates

Most animals (97 percent) are invertebrates. Some have a hard shell or outer skeleton.

Vertebrates

Vertebrates are split into five smaller groups: mammals, birds, reptiles, amphibians and fishes.

Coats and armour

You are a hairy animal, like other mammals. Other animal groups have different body coverings. Birds have feathers, amphibians have smooth skin, and reptiles and most fish have scales.

Skin suit

An animal's skin is like a waterproof suit, which protects its body from damage and disease.

Always in armour

Scales made from hard skin, or horn, protect the bodies of some animals like suits of armour.

Hide and seek

Colours and patterns help some animals to play hide and seek! Others use them to stand out from the crowd.

In plain sight

Many animals that are good at hiding from predators have colours or patterns that match their background. This is called camouflage.

Don't eat me!

Animals that are poisonous or taste nasty often have bright colours to warn predators not to eat them.

Baby animals are often well camouflaged to protect them while they are small.

Colour change

Some animals are experts at changing colour, either to blend in or to scare off predators. Chameleons and octopuses change colour as their mood or environment changes.

Made for moving

Most animals move to find food or shelter, escape danger, find a mate and care for young. Their bodies are built for movement, whether they run, fly or swim.

I can only sprint at top speed for about 30 seconds before I get tired.

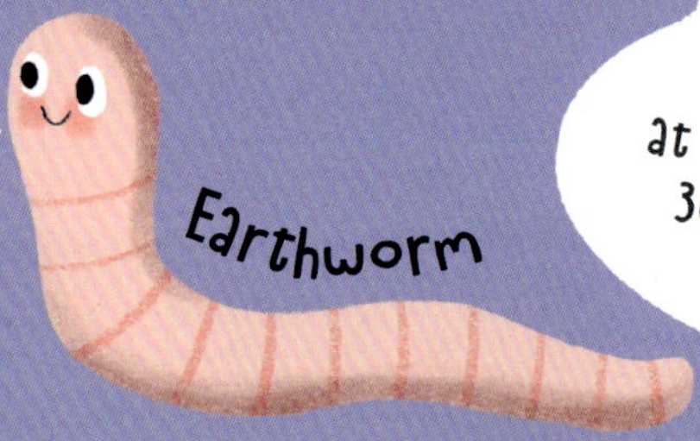

Some animals move around on land without any legs at all!

Basilisk lizards can walk on water!

Fishy tales

Most fish swim by bending their body, or just their tail, from side to side. Fast fish have powerful muscles and a smooth shape to help them glide through water.

Speed champion

Many predators chase their prey. The cheetah is the fastest land animal over short distances, sprinting at up to 100 kilometres an hour.

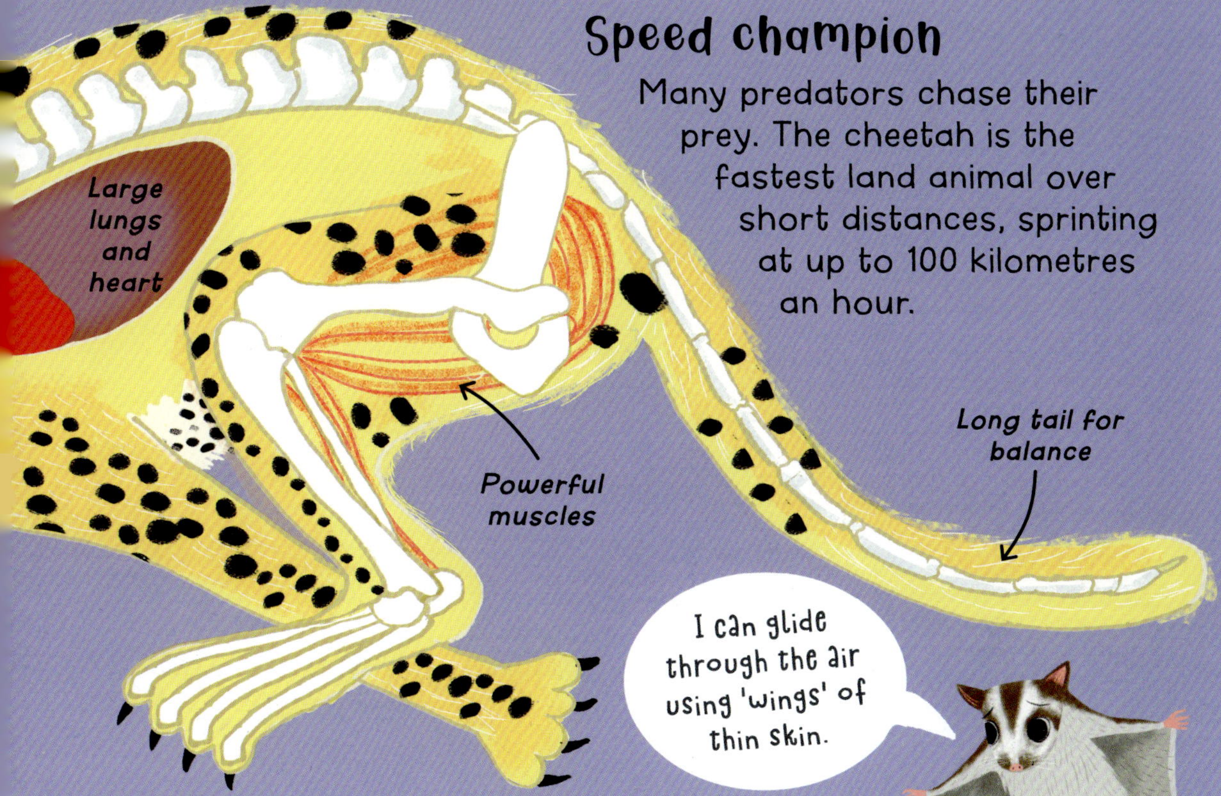

Great traveller

Some animals cover very long distances on journeys called migrations. The Arctic tern flies from the top of the world to the bottom and back each year, avoiding winter altogether.

Newborn babies

Baby animals either hatch out of eggs or are born from their mother's body. Mothers that give birth to babies protect and feed them inside their bodies until they are ready to be born.

Cosy nests

Animals that lay eggs often build nests to keep them safe. Nile crocodiles bury their eggs in sandy nests close to water.

Shark eggs are protected by special cases that are often called mermaid's purses.

Growing up

Some young animals, such as snakes or orangutans, look like their parents. Others, such as frogs, look very different at first. They change as they grow up.

6 The froglet grows into an adult frog.

5 The tadpole has become a froglet, and has left the water.

3 The tadpole gets bigger. Its back legs start to grow.

4 The front legs grow. Over time, the tail gets shorter.

2 A tiny tadpole hatches from each egg. It can breathe underwater through flaps called gills.

1 Frog eggs are called frogspawn. Female frogs lay them in large clumps underwater.

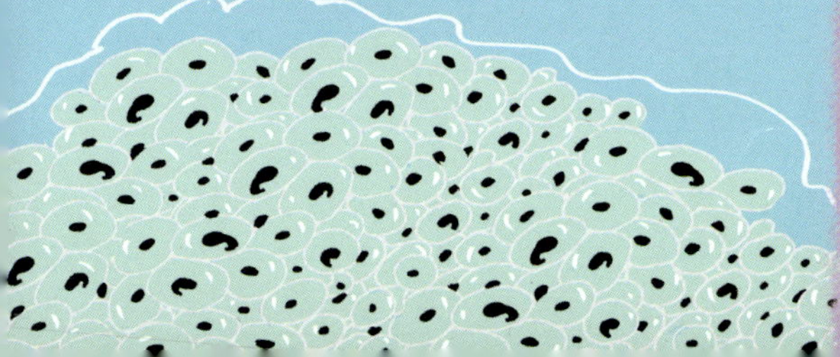

Pocket baby

Animals with pouches, such as kangaroos and wombats, are called marsupials. Their babies are tiny when they are born and grow slowly inside their mother's pouch.

Hungry animals

All animals need to eat to live. Omnivores, such as foxes, eat almost anything. Herbivores, such as hares, eat only plants. Carnivores like eagles just eat meat. Food chains show how animals are linked by what they eat.

Hares have teeth that never stop growing. Gnawing on tough plants wears them down.

Animal cutlery

To break up solid food, some animals use their teeth or jaws and some birds use their bills. Many insects suck up liquid food with special mouthparts.

Giant anteaters flick out their long tongues at up to 160 times per minute as they feed.

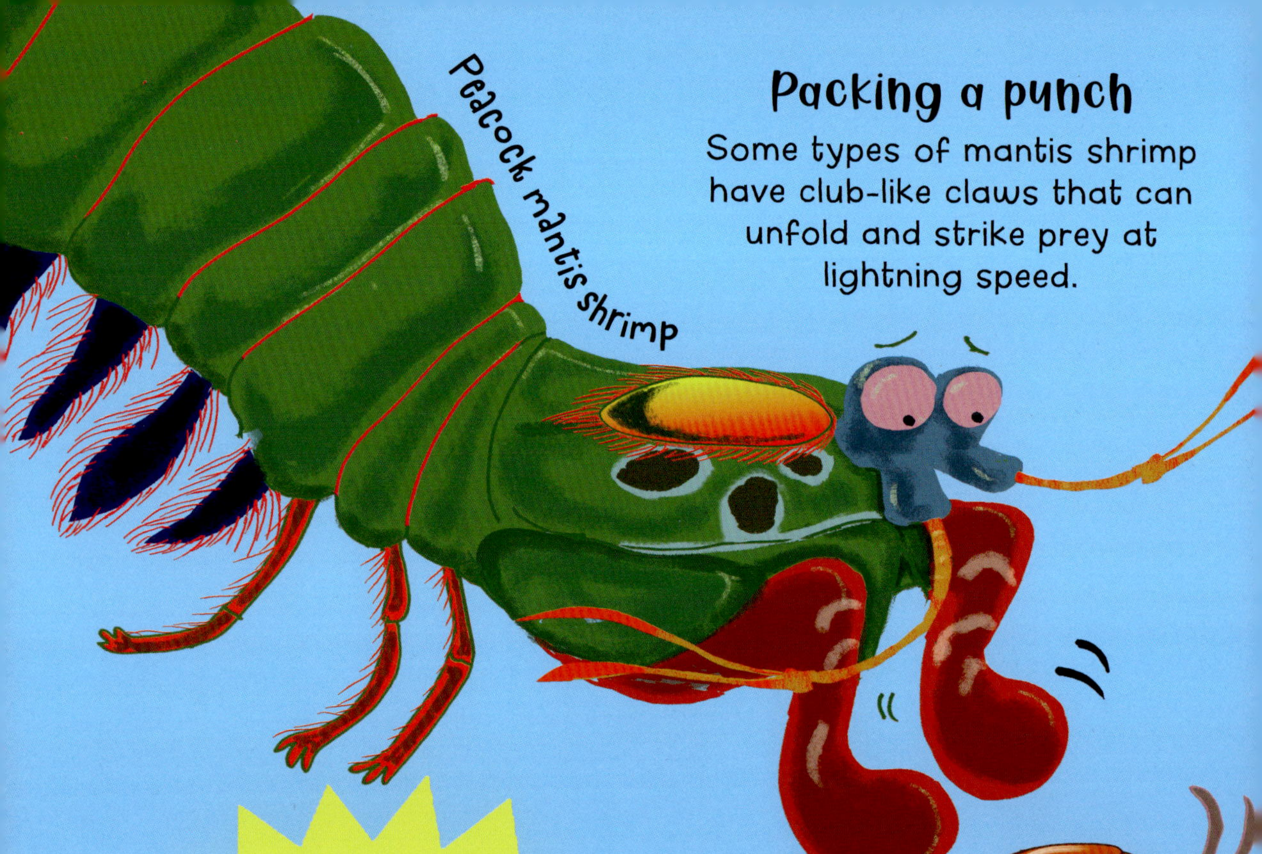

Packing a punch

Some types of mantis shrimp have club-like claws that can unfold and strike prey at lightning speed.

A mantis shrimp's punch is so powerful it can smash glass!

Predators and prey

Predators hunt, catch and eat other animals, which are called their prey. They use weapons such as big teeth, powerful jaws, sharp claws, sticky tongues and poison.

Hidden danger

Cunning predators may set traps. Some trapdoor spiders grab their prey from behind a kind of door at their burrow entrance.

Trapdoor spider

Fighting back

Prey animals defend themselves with teeth, claws or spines. They may also use tricks. The frilled lizard opens its neck frill to look big and scary to predators.

Super senses

Animals usually collect information about their surroundings using their senses of sight, hearing, smell, taste and touch. Keen senses help animals to survive.

Lots of lenses

A dragonfly has enormous eyes. Each eye is made up of about 30,000 tiny lenses joined together.

Fantastic feelers

Some animals sense the world in a different way from us. Butterflies and moths smell with their feelers, called antennae. They also taste with their feet.

Invisible ears

Mammals have ear flaps outside their head. Other animals just have inside ears. The dish-like shape of a barn owl's face helps to direct sounds to its inside ears.

Chameleons can move each eye in a different direction at the same time to see all around.

Safe homes

A home can give animals shelter, protection from predators, and a place to store food and have a family. Many animals build their homes.

Weaving wonder

Male weaverbirds make a nest by weaving together grass, stems and leaves. The nests have narrow entrances that face down, so predators can't get in.

The biggest bald eagle nest weighed more than a rhino!

Champion digger

Animals that build underground homes are very good diggers. Moles dig tunnels with their long nails and spade-like paws, which are linked to strong chest muscles.

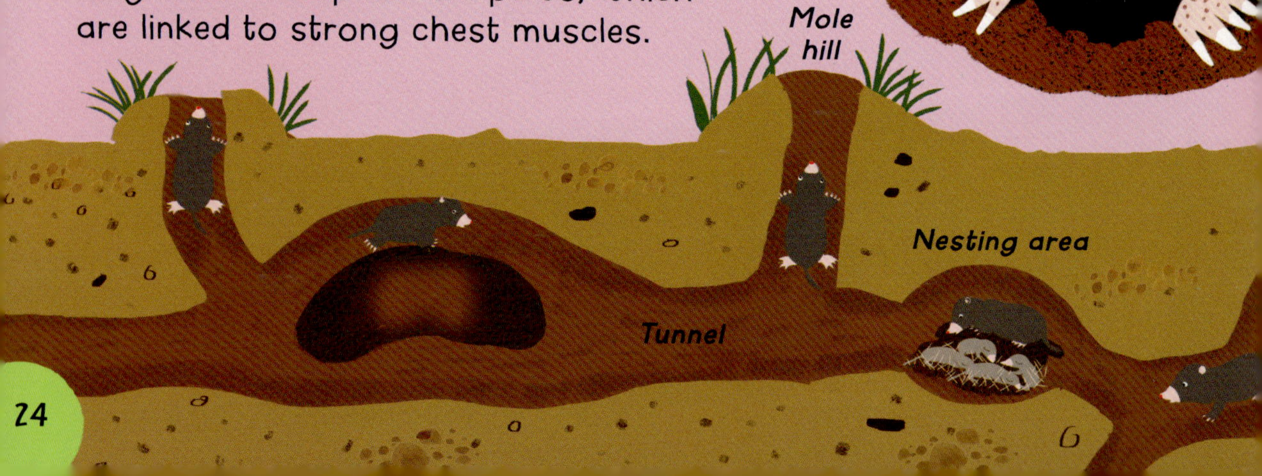

Water worlds

Animals thrive in freshwater habitats. There is plenty of food in rivers and lakes and lots of places for birds and mammals to nest and raise their young.

Tiny insects called pond skaters can walk on water without sinking.

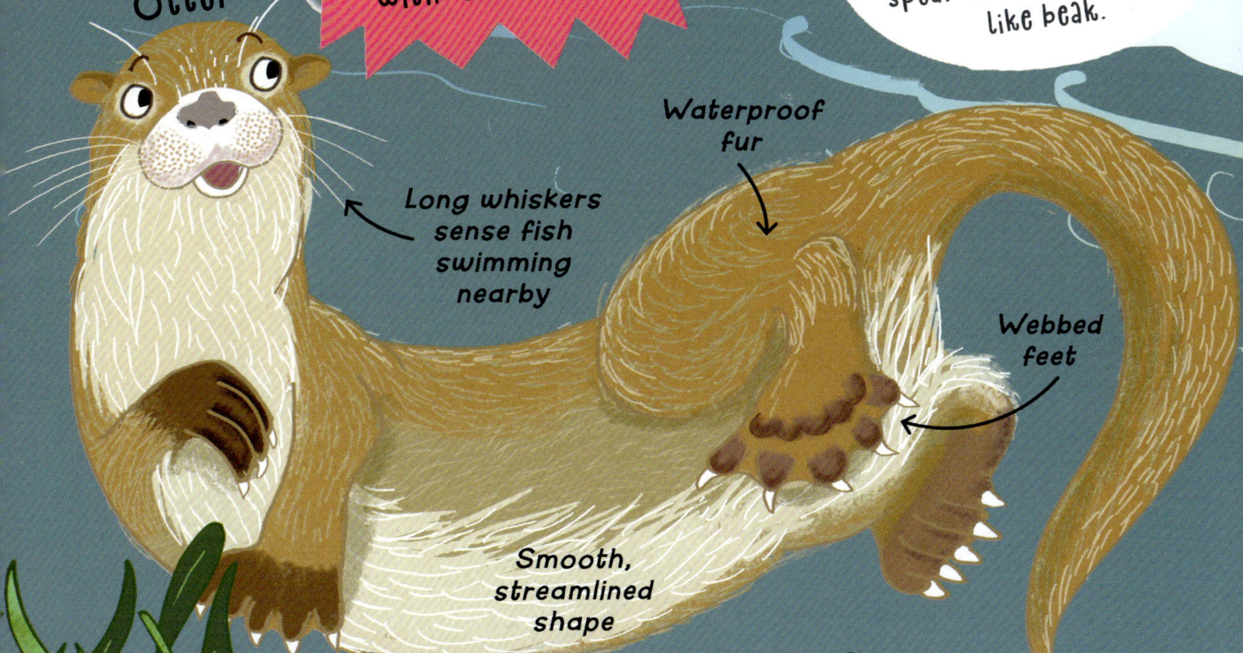

Flipper feet

Some water animals, such as otters, have skin between their toes. They use their webbed feet to push against the water and swim faster, rather like a person wearing flippers.

Night life

If you sleep during the day and are active at night, you're nocturnal. Animals that are nocturnal can avoid daytime heat and predators. There is also less competition for food, as there are fewer nocturnal animals than daytime ones.

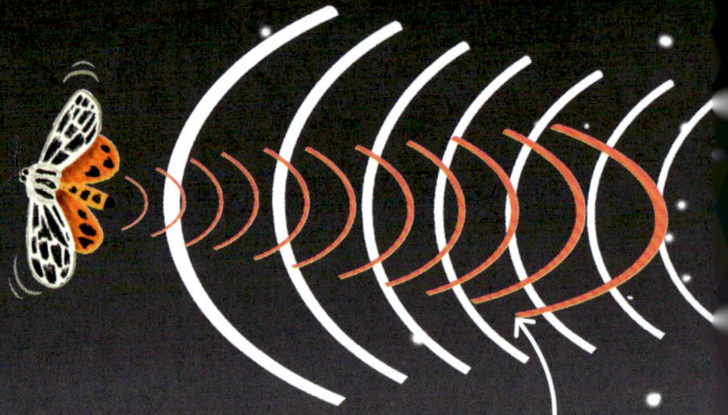

Each spotted hyena has its own unique whooping call. It can use it to find other members of its clan in the dark.

Bouncing back

Bats make high-pitched sounds and listen for the echoes that bounce back from objects. This is called echolocation. It helps the bat to hunt.

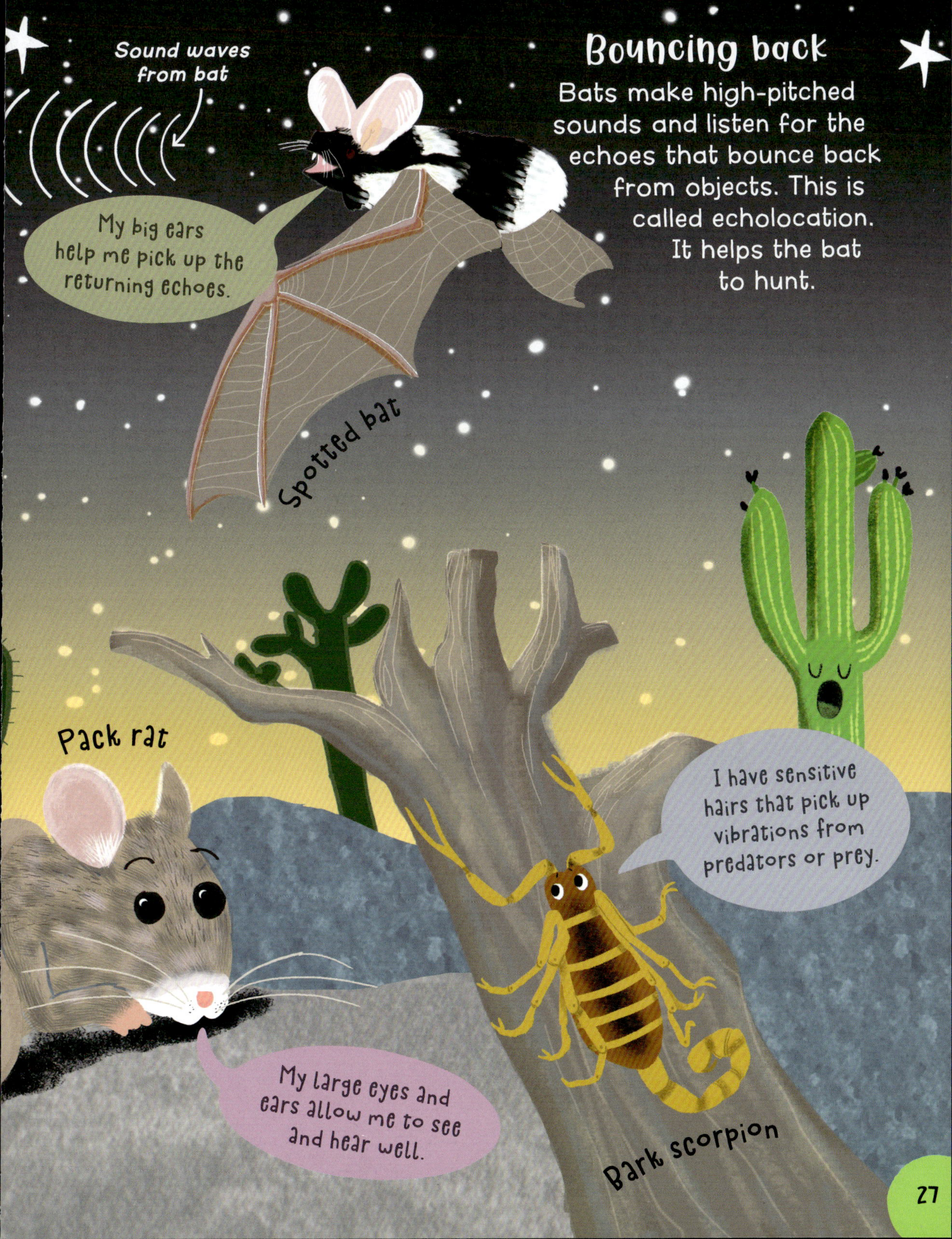

Living in groups

Animals that live in groups help each other to find food, watch out for danger and bring up the young. Group living also helps animals to cope with changes.

Elephant seal pups

Safety in numbers

Some animals, such as penguins and seals, live in groups only for the breeding season. Many adults can keep a sharper lookout for predators.

Watch and learn

Young animals in a group learn by copying the adults. Chimps learn how to get termites out of a mound by watching an adult 'fish' with a stem or twig.

Worker termites collect food and clean the nest
The queen termite lays thousands of eggs a day
Soldier termites defend the nest using their big jaws
Up to five million termites live inside one termite mound.

During the harsh Antarctic winter, **emperor penguins** form giant huddles for warmth. They take turns to be on the outside!

Out in the cold

In Earth's coldest places, animals have thick fur or feathers and fatty blubber to keep them warm. Small, round ears also help to stop an animal's body heat escaping.

Ice fish have a chemical 'anti-freeze' in their blood. This keeps them from freezing solid in Antarctic waters.

Too hot to handle

In hot, dry deserts, many animals hide from the daytime heat and get most of their water from their food. Desert animals such as camels can go without food and water for a long time.

Scorpions can survive without water for several months.

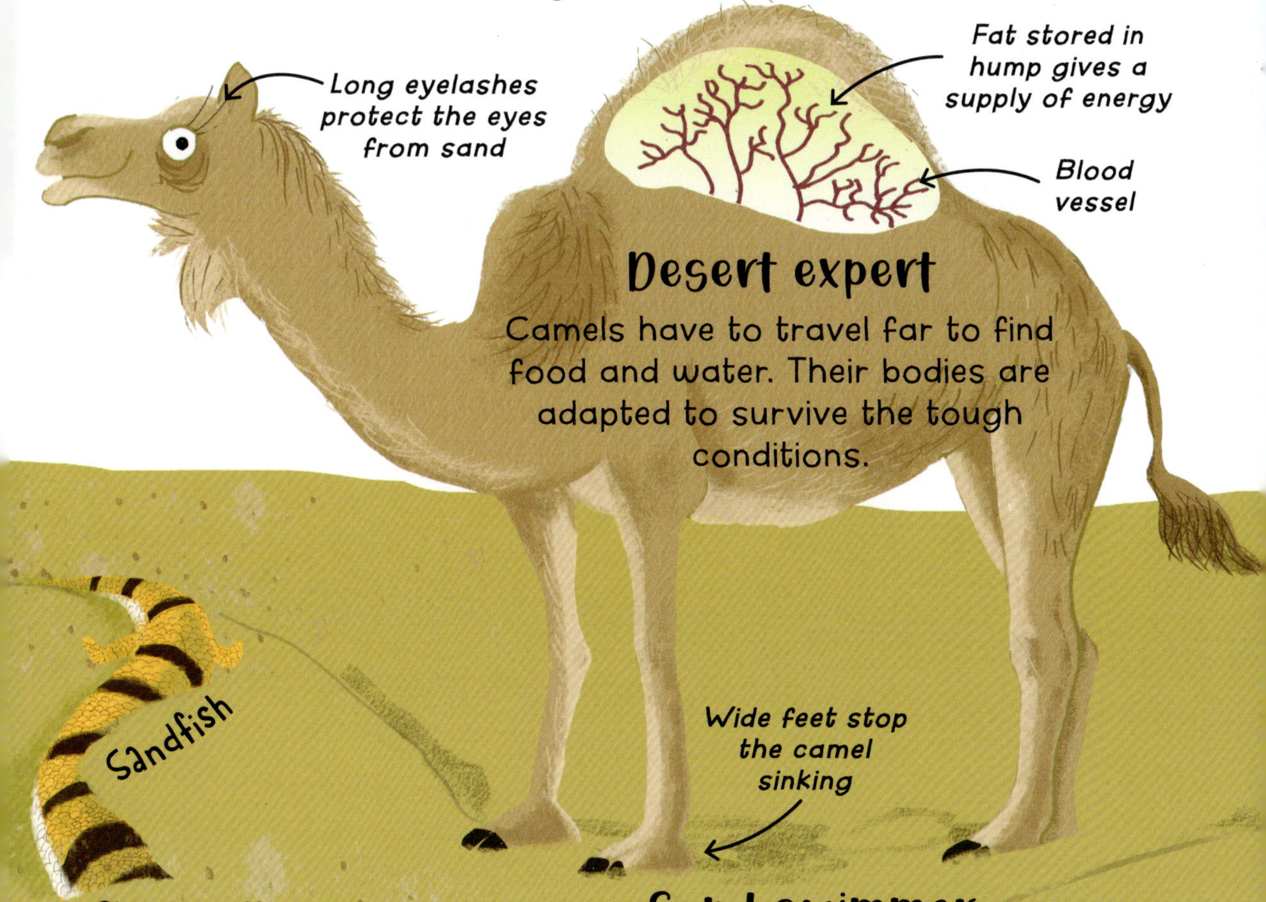

Desert expert

Camels have to travel far to find food and water. Their bodies are adapted to survive the tough conditions.

Sand swimmer

It's hard to move across very hot, soft sand, so the sandfish (a type of lizard) burrows underneath and swims through it like a fish through water.

DINOSAURS

What are dinosaurs?

Dinosaurs are ancient land-dwelling reptiles that once roamed the Earth. They died out millions of years ago, but we can learn about them from the traces they left behind.

Over 800 different types of dinosaurs have been discovered so far.

What's in a name?

Dinosaurs are often named after how they look, where they were found or who found them. *Herrerasaurus* was named after goat herder Victorino Herrera who first found this dinosaur in Argentina in 1959.

We don't know exactly what dinosaurs looked like or what colours they were.

The first dinosaurs

These amazing creatures are thought to have lived over 230 million years ago. Most early dinosaurs moved around on two legs.

Small and speedy

Eoraptor was a small but fast two-legged dinosaur. It was about one metre long and weighed 10 kilograms – about the same as a small dog.

Standing tall

Plateosaurus was a plant-eater that could stand on its back legs to reach leaves way up high.

Group hunter

Coelophysis could grow to be about as tall as you. This early dinosaur lived and hunted in large groups.

Dinosaur skeletons are really rare. People were amazed when 100 *Coelophysis* skeletons were found all together in the USA in 1947.

When did dinosaurs live?

Dinosaurs lived on Earth between 235 and 66 million years ago in a time known as the Age of Dinosaurs. This is split into three parts, called the Triassic, Jurassic and Cretaceous periods.

JURASSIC

This middle time period was between 200 and 145 million years ago.

TRIASSIC

Dinosaurs first appeared on Earth in Triassic times, between 250 and 200 million years ago.

One big home

When dinosaurs first arrived, all of the land on Earth was clumped together in one big mass called Pangaea. Over time, the land drifted apart, taking dinosaurs to different parts of the planet.

CRETACEOUS

Lots of dinosaurs lived in Jurassic times, including the gigantic plant-eating sauropods.

Huge meat-eaters and large armoured plant-eaters roamed Earth in the Cretaceous Period.

No single type of dinosaur lived throughout the Age of Dinosaurs. Many different kinds came and went.

The Cretaceous Period, between 145 and 66 million years ago, was the height of the Age of Dinosaurs.

Great grazers

The prehistoric world was packed with plants. More than half of all known dinosaur species were plant-eaters.

Slow and strong

Stegosaurus was built like a tank. It weighed up to 3.5 tonnes and moved slowly, eating mostly twigs and leaves.

Spiky thumb

Iguanodon could walk on four legs, but rise up on two to reach taller bushes and trees.

Mighty meat-eaters

Many dinosaurs hunted other creatures. Some relied on speed and quick reactions to catch creatures. Others used their big size and brute strength.

Spinosaurus

Longer than a school bus, this big beast liked hunting in water. It gobbled up huge fish, spearing them with its long jaws full of sharp teeth.

Super-sized sauropods

These dinosaurs were huge plant-eaters. They all had long tails to balance out the long necks that they needed to reach plants way up high.

Apatosaurus had to eat 400 kilograms of food a day to survive.

Heavyweight champion

Argentinosaurus was a 35-metre-long giant and one of the heaviest dinosaurs. It weighed about 70 tonnes, more than five times the size of *T rex*.

Diplodocus' long tail was more than half the total length of its body

Spiny plant-eater

Diplodocus was a 26-metre-long dinosaur weighing about 20 tonnes. It used its peg-shaped teeth to strip leaves off of branches.

Stony stomach

Apatosaurus didn't chew its food but instead swallowed it whole. Like many plant-eaters, it also ate large stones that stayed in its stomach and helped grind the food down.

Teeth and claws

Dinosaur experts love looking at teeth and claws. These things help to tell us lots about how dinosaurs lived and the sorts of things they liked to eat.

Types of teeth

Dino teeth were well-matched to the different sorts of food that dinosaurs ate.

Razor claws

Claws on dinosaurs' hands and feet were used for attack, defence and to gather food.

Therizinosaurus had huge slashing claws on its hands up to one metre in length!

Horns and armour

Some plant-eating dinosaurs were slow and heavy and couldn't run away from predators. Luckily, they were protected by heavy armour, and some had long horns or clubs too.

Triceratops had one of the biggest dinosaur heads – almost a third of its body length.

Three-horned face

Triceratops was enormous – up to 9 metres long and 3 metres high. A thick, scaly skin and three horns helped protect it from attack.

Bone head

With a big bony dome on its head and a crown of short spikes, *Pachycephalosaurus* butted away predators or rivals.

Ankylosaurus had armour so thick that an attacker could break its teeth trying to bite through it!

Nests and eggs

Dinosaurs hatched from eggs, just like birds and crocodiles today. The smallest dinosaur eggs were just 1.8 centimetres long but others were up to 60 centimetres in length.

Good parents

Troodon parents half buried their eggs in mud in round nests. They then sat over the eggs to keep them warm until they hatched.

Dino babies

Most baby dinosaurs had to feed and defend themselves as soon as they hatched. Baby *Maiasaura* were lucky. They had parents who cared for them until they could look after themselves.

Maiasaura grew up fast. By their eighth birthday, they could weigh 2.3 tonnes!

Caring colonies

Plant-eating *Maiasaura* lived together in herds and raised their young in colonies. They brought food to their babies while they were still in the nest.

On the move

Just like buffaloes or zebras today, some dinosaurs lived in large herds. This helped to protect individuals from attack by fierce meat-eaters.

Happy herds

We know dinosaurs moved in herds by studying groups of their footprints and skeletons that have all been found in the same place. These *Parasaurolophus* were big dinosaurs that lived in large herds.

A vast herd of thousands of *Centrosaurus* skeletons has been found in Canada.

Young *Parasaurolophus* walked on two legs. As they grew up and got heavier they often walked on all four.

T rex terror!

Tyrannosaurus rex is one of the most famous and fierce dinosaurs of all. *T rex* hunted many other dinosaurs but may also have feasted on dead animals that it found.

Jaws of awe

T rex's jaws were 1.2 metres long – about as long as you are tall! When opened wide, its jaws revealed 60 long, sharp, cone-shaped teeth.

A T rex skeleton found in 1990, called Sue, was sold for $8.3 million!

T rex teenagers got heavier fast. They could add 2 kilograms to their weight every day.

The end of the dinosaurs

Dinosaurs lived on Earth until about 66 million years ago when they disappeared. This is what we think happened...

An asteroid streaks across the sky.

❶ The last dinosaurs

Around 66 million years ago, dinosaurs were still thriving on land. Big beasts like *Triceratops*, *Ankylosaurus* and mighty *T rex* were all still alive.

❷ Impact!

An asteroid (a large rock from space) struck Earth. It sent huge clouds of dust into the air, blocking out the Sun and making Earth much colder and darker than before.

③ Dying out

Earth went through climate change for many years. Lots of plants died out and so did many creatures, including all of the dinosaurs.

Many volcanoes also erupted, adding to the damage.

④ Survivors

Some creatures survived including crocodiles, turtles, snakes and birds. New animals appeared after the dinosaurs including monkeys, wild cats and us – humans!

Seeds survived, providing food for birds after the asteroid impact.

SPACE

Space is huge!

Space is absolutely everything that exists beyond our planet. It's HUGE! All of space is called the Universe. Scientists think it is very old and began 13.8 thousand million years ago. So what can we find in space?

The Moon is small and rocky

Planets are balls of rock or gas that travel around a star. We live on planet Earth

Some stars are hundreds of times bigger than our Sun.

The Sun

The Sun is our nearest star. Stars are big balls of gas. They are usually very hot.

Space measure

Light travels super fast. It can circle Earth 15 times in just two seconds. Scientists use how far light travels in one year to measure big distances in space. One light year is...

9,500,000,000,000 km!

Meet the neighbours

Welcome to the Solar System – Earth's neighbourhood. It contains eight planets that travel round a star called the Sun. The oval-shaped path the planets take through space is called an orbit.

Mooning around

Moons are rocky bodies that orbit a planet instead of the Sun. There are more than 200 moons in our Solar System.

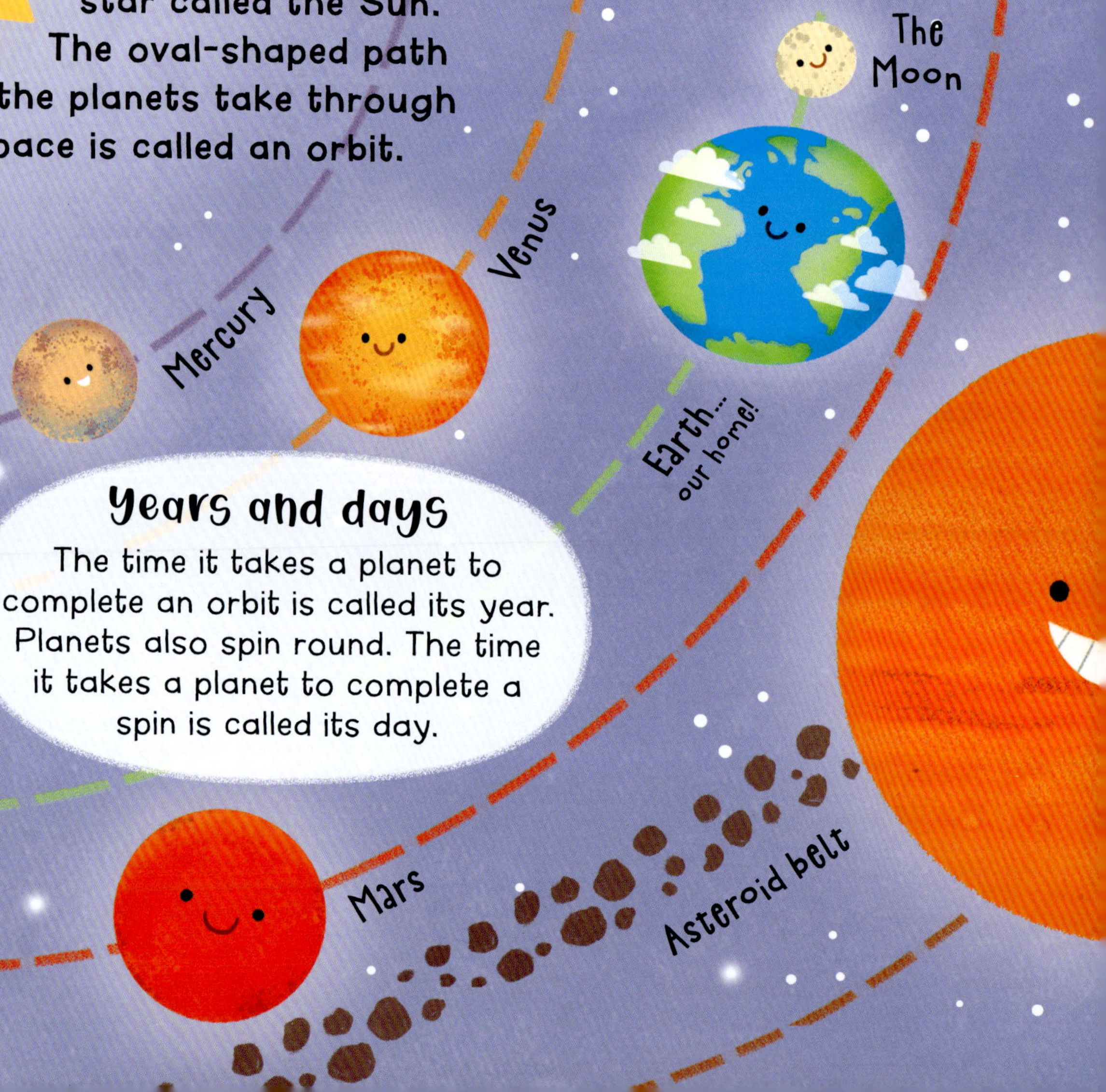

Years and days

The time it takes a planet to complete an orbit is called its year. Planets also spin round. The time it takes a planet to complete a spin is called its day.

The asteroid belt contains lots of rocks that also orbit the Sun.

A year on Saturn is 29.5 times longer than a year on Earth. It lasts 10,755 days!

Jupiter

Jupiter is the biggest planet in our Solar System.

Saturn

Neptune

Uranus

If the Sun was the size of a basketball, Earth would be a small pea and Jupiter a table tennis ball.

Sunny stuff

The Sun is our nearest star. It is about 150 million kilometres from Earth. Despite being so far away, its energy gives us light and warmth. Without the Sun, life could not exist on Earth.

It's a gas

The Sun is a giant ball of flaming gases, mostly hydrogen and helium. It is as wide as 109 planet Earths in a row.

Solar eclipse

Sometimes, the Moon blocks the view of the Sun from Earth. This event is called an eclipse, and parts of the world become dark. An eclipse only lasts a few minutes.

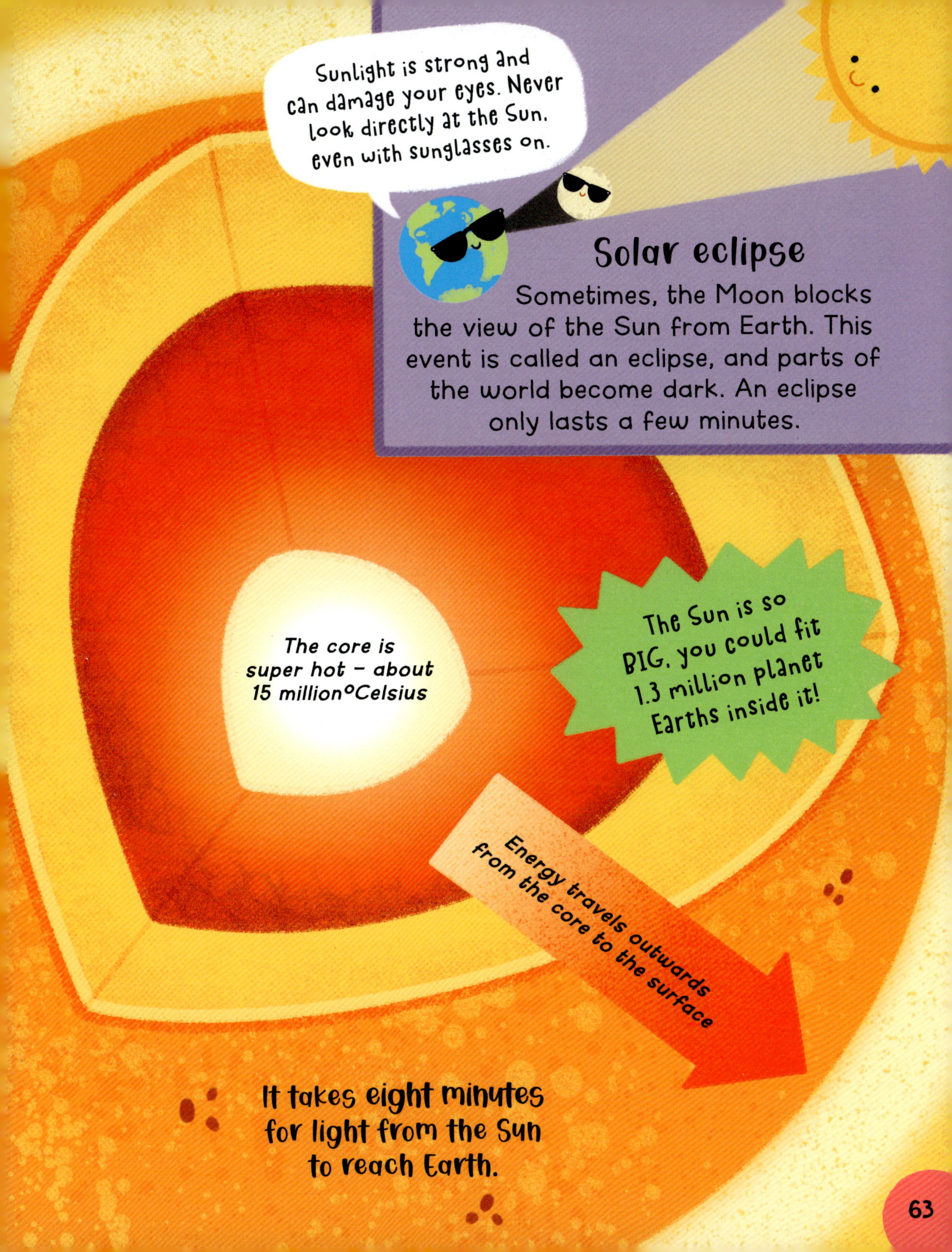

Our planet

Earth is the fifth biggest planet in the Solar System. It receives just the right amount of heat from the Sun for life to flourish.

Earth's atmosphere

Earth is surrounded by a blanket of gases. This is the atmosphere, and it gives us air to breathe. The gases also trap the Sun's heat, keeping Earth warm.

Earth is kept in its orbit by **gravity**, a special force that pulls objects together.

Earth spins at about 1670 kilometres an hour. That's about twice the speed of a passenger jet plane.

Our orbiting rock

The Moon is our nearest neighbour, but it is still 384,400 kilometres away. At just over a quarter of the size of Earth, it is the only place in space that humans have visited.

Apollo astronauts landed on the Moon in a lunar module

Moon landings

Apollo spacecraft took American astronauts to the Moon between 1969 and 1972. A total of 12 astronauts walked on the Moon's surface. Neil Armstrong was the first person to step onto the Moon after a three day journey through space.

The big whack

Scientists think the Moon was formed when a giant object crashed into Earth four billion years ago. All the rocks thrown up by the crash clumped together to create the Moon.

Gravity is much weaker on the Moon. This makes it easier to take big, bounding strides, even in heavy spacesuits.

Lots of machines have travelled to the Moon, including China's Jade Rabbit 2 in 2019.

There's no wind or water on the Moon. So, footprints made by Apollo astronauts are still there!

The Moon's surface is rocky and dusty

Closest to the Sun

Hot, rocky planets Mercury and Venus are closest to the Sun. Mercury is covered in craters where rocks crashed into it in the past, and it has hardly any atmosphere. Venus is covered by thick layers of gases.

Speedy planet

Mercury moves through space at over 170,000 kilometres an hour. That's more than 47 kilometres every second! It orbits the Sun every 88 days. Earth takes over four times as long.

The Caloris Basin crater on Mercury would stretch from London to Rome – it's 1500 kilometres wide.

Mercury is the smallest planet in our Solar System, at 4879 kilometres wide.

Volcanic Venus

Volcanoes pump out gases that form a thick blanket around Venus. These gases trap heat, making the planet the hottest in our Solar System. Its surface is around 462°Celsius. That's 15 times hotter than a summer's day on Earth.

Mission Mars

Planet Mars is just over half the size of Earth. It has two small moons called Phobos and Deimos. Mars is much colder than Earth. Its average temperature is -60°Celsius. Brrr!

Mars lies between 54–401 million kilometres from Earth.

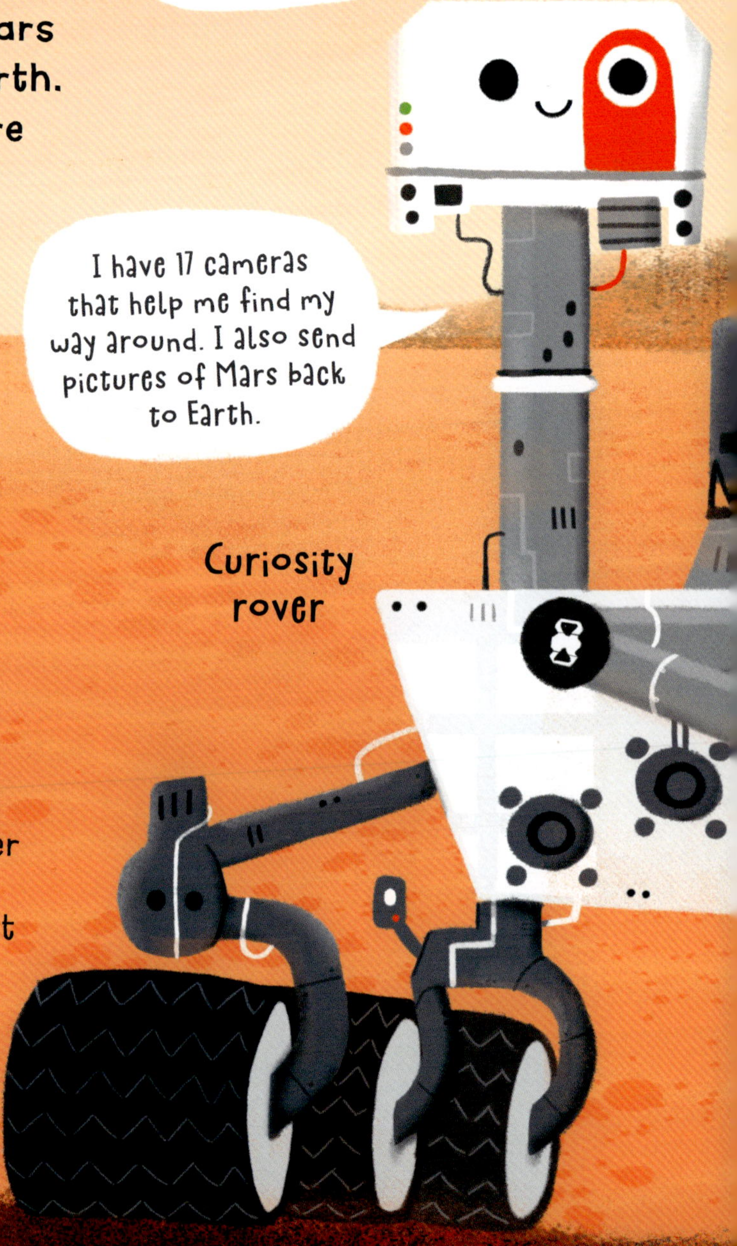

Robot explorers

Scientists wonder if life ever existed on Mars. Several robot rovers have been sent there to investigate. One day, people may even be sent to visit.

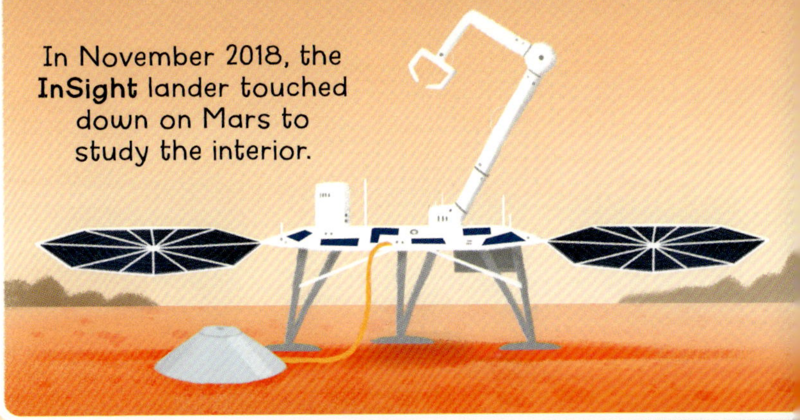

In November 2018, the **InSight** lander touched down on Mars to study the interior.

Olympus Mons volcano is 25,000 metres tall – three times taller than Mount Everest

Transmitter sends back lots of photos to Earth

Valles Marineris is a giant canyon on Mars, which would stretch across the United States of America!

In 2021 a mini helicopter called Ingenuity arrived on Mars with the Perseverance rover. Ingenuity became the first vehicle to fly on another planet.

What else is in space?

Other objects are found in our Solar System. Sometimes, these can be spotted in the night sky.

Ceres is the biggest object in the asteroid belt. It is more than 960 kilometres wide.

Asteroids

These rocky objects orbit the Sun. Millions are found in a belt between Mars and Jupiter, and more than a million measure over one kilometre in diameter. Scientists think they may be pieces of a planet that never formed.

Comets

These 'dirty snowballs' orbit the Sun and are made up of ice, dust and rock. As they get near to the Sun, they heat up and some of the comet breaks away. It forms a long tail that trails behind.

Meteorites

Chunks of rock, metal and dust drifting through space are called meteoroids. These sometimes burn up in Earth's atmosphere to form a spectacular meteor shower. If one reaches the ground, it is renamed a meteorite.

Mighty Jupiter

A huge planet, Jupiter is the biggest in our Solar System. It is 2.5 times more massive than all the other planets put together. Jupiter is about five times farther from the Sun than Earth.

Gas giant

Jupiter is made up of a mixture of gases. This means it has no solid surface for a spacecraft to land on. It is 11 times the diameter of Earth.

Moon hunter

No one knew Jupiter had moons until Italian scientist Galileo (1564–1642) discovered four in 1610. Scientists have since discovered more than 70 further moons orbiting Jupiter.

Ganymede is the largest moon in the entire Solar System. It's actually bigger than the planet Mercury.
Ganymede
Darker stripes of gas across the planet are known as belts
Lighter bands on Jupiter's surface are called zones
The Great Red Spot storm has been raging not for a week or two, but for at least 350 years!
Callisto
The Galileo probe visited Jupiter in 1995 after a six year journey from Earth

Farthest from the Sun

The three planets farthest from the Sun are all much bigger than Earth and made of gas. They are also very, very chilly. The surface of Uranus is about -200°Celsius. That's over ten times colder than your kitchen freezer.

Saturn may be huge, but it is made of light gases. It's the only planet that would float in water... if you could find a bowl big enough!

Far, far away

Saturn is 9.5 times further away from the Sun than Earth. It takes 10,700 days (29.5 years) to complete an orbit around the Sun. Uranus and Neptune are even more distant. Neptune takes 164 years to complete an orbit.

Neptune is 49,000 kilometres wide.

Uranus has unusual seasons because it is tilted. A winter around its north pole lasts 21 years.

Giant galaxies

Stars are rarely found on their own. They are usually part of a massive collection of dust, gas, planets and other stars called a galaxy. Our galaxy is called the Milky Way – it contains at least 100 billion stars.

Some galaxies are cannibals. They crash into and gobble up other, smaller galaxies.

Our galaxy

The Milky Way is over 100,000 light years wide and shaped like a spiral. Its curving arms each contain millions of stars. The Milky Way is about 1000 light years thick, with a thicker bulge in the middle.

Other galaxies

Some galaxies are far bigger than the Milky Way. The Malin 1 spiral galaxy, for example, is around six times bigger. Other galaxies are a different shape to the Milky Way.

Our whole Solar System orbits around the centre of the Milky Way. The orbit takes a long, long time – about 230 million years!

HUMAN BODY

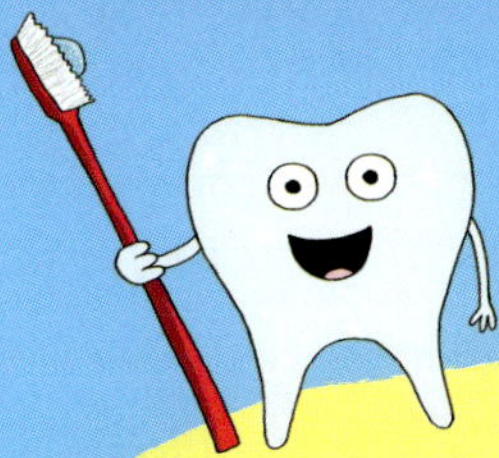

From top to toe

The human body comes in lots of shapes and sizes. But most bodies are made up of the same parts, which do the same jobs.

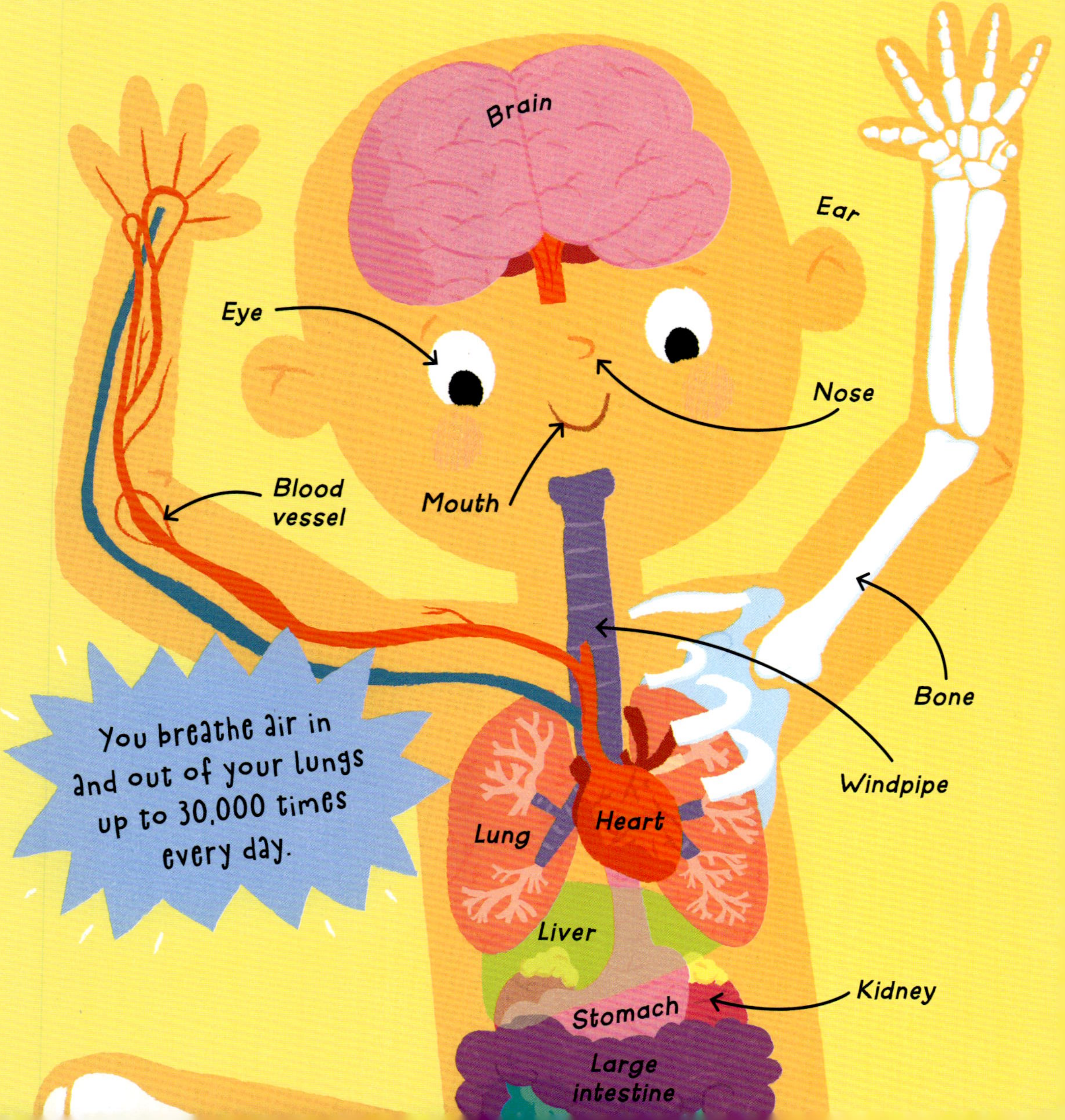

You have lots of bones inside you! Together they provide your body with a strong framework.

More than half of the bones in your body are in your hands and feet.

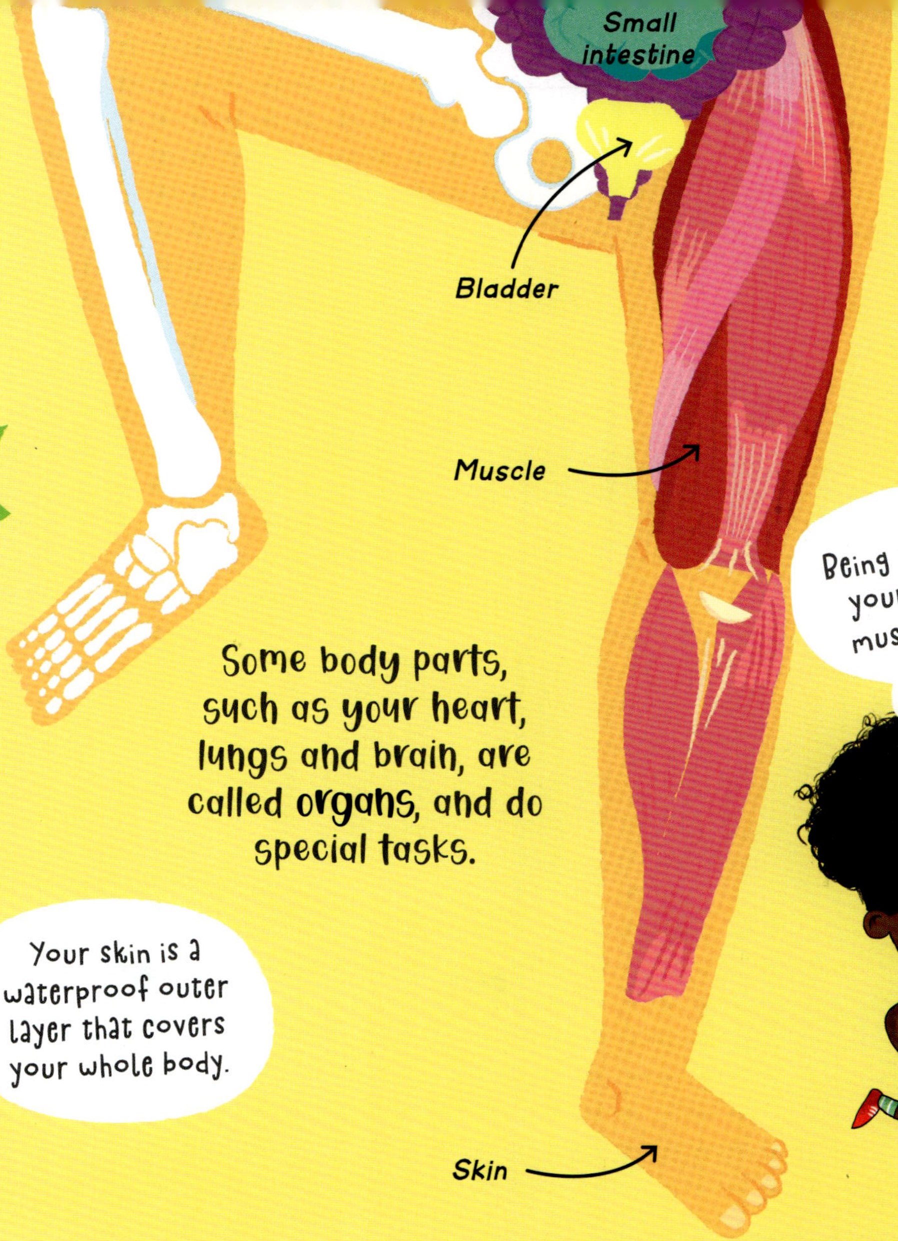

Some body parts, such as your heart, lungs and brain, are called **organs**, and do special tasks.

Your skin is a waterproof outer layer that covers your whole body.

Being active makes your bones and muscles strong.

Outside in

You're wearing a coat even when you have no clothes on! Your skin is a thin, stretchy, waterproof covering that protects your body.

Sweaty stuff

Your skin releases sweat, which is mostly water. Sweating helps keep you cool. You sweat more from different parts of your body than others.

Outer protection

Skin stops germs getting into your body. It is also packed with special cells called sensors, which give you your sense of touch.

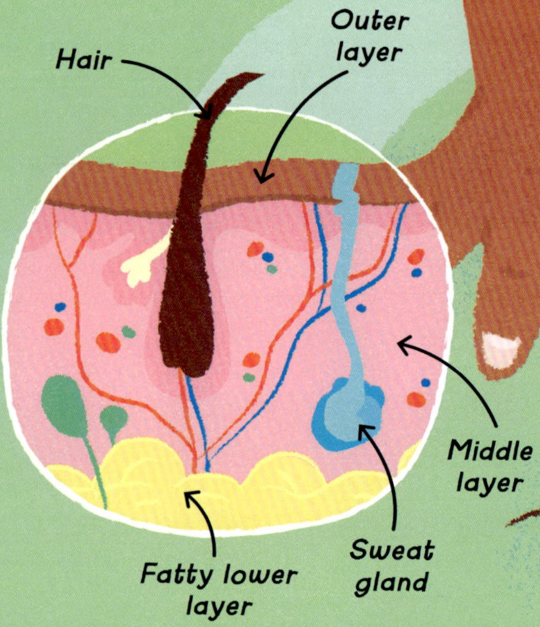

Hairy!

You have around 100,000 hairs on your head. Millions more grow out of your skin elsewhere.

Harmful rays from the Sun can damage your skin. That's why you should wear sunblock.

Fingernails grow by about one centimetre every three months.

Nailed it

Fingernails give your fingertips protection. They're made from the same materials as hair.

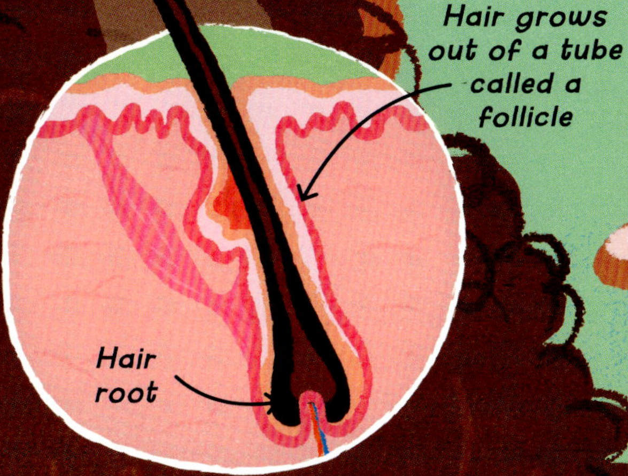

Hair can be straight, wavy or curly

Super skeleton

Your skeleton is made of more than 200 bones. It supports your body, helps you move, protects extra-special parts such as your brain, and grows as you grow.

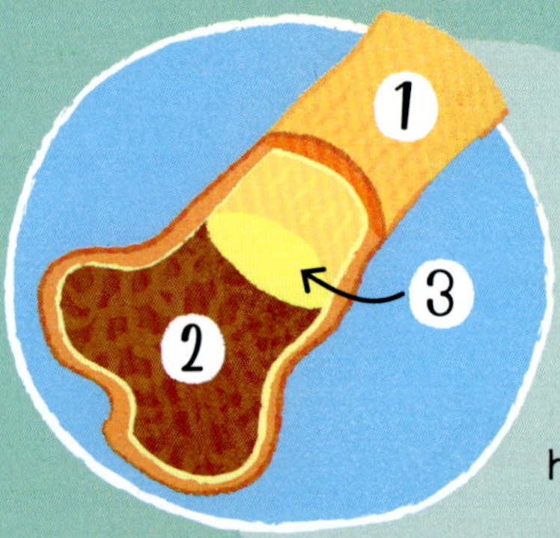

Inside a bone
A bone's outside (1) is hard and tough. Inside (2), it looks like honeycomb, with many tiny holes, so it's strong but light. In the middle is the jelly-like marrow (3).

Move it

A joint is where two or more bones meet. There are lots of different types of joint, and they help you to move in different ways.

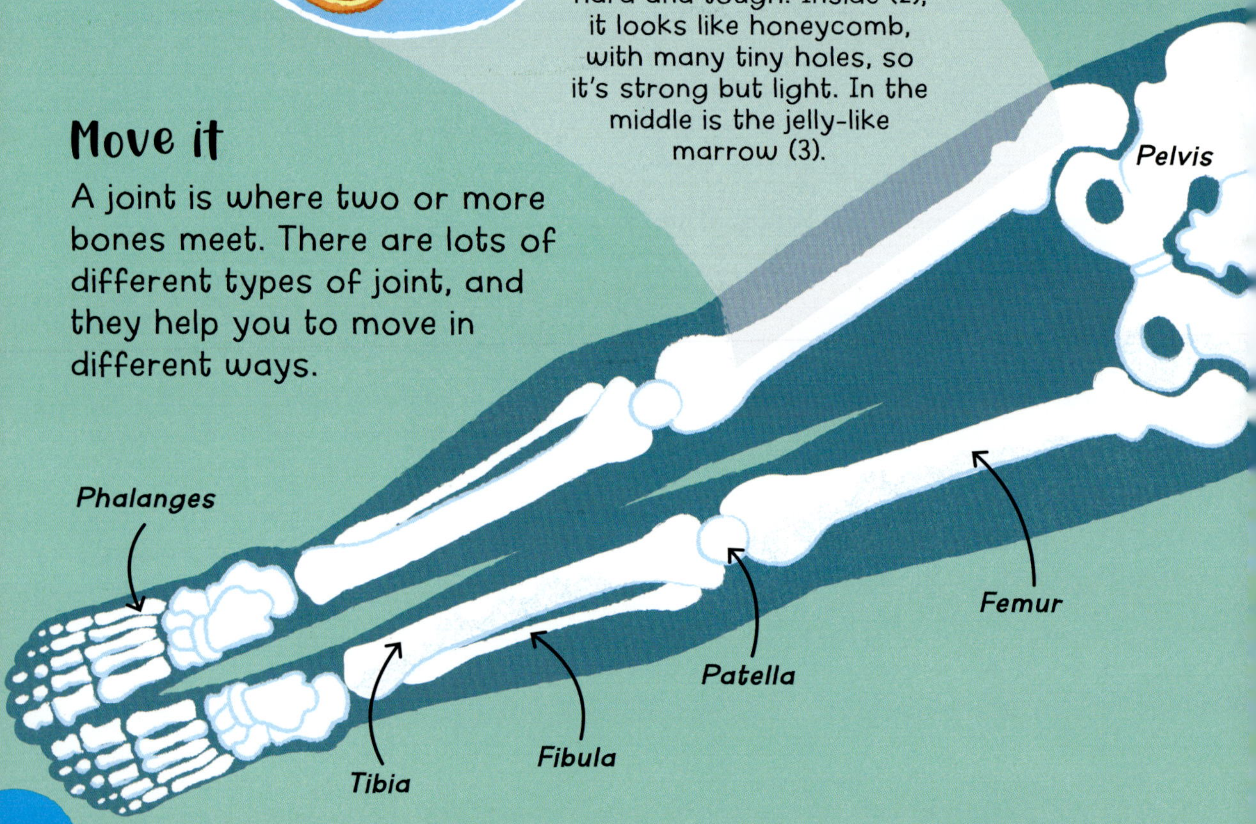

How tall are you?

Everyone's skeleton is a little bit different. It is what gives shape to your body, and can be tall or short.

From four to ten years old, most children grow around 6 centimetres taller each year.

Without bones you would collapse like a **pile of jelly!**

Your thigh bone (femur) is the longest bone in your body.

Magic muscles

There are more than 600 muscles in your body. Every move you make, from blinking your eye to lifting a bag, is made by these power-packed parts.

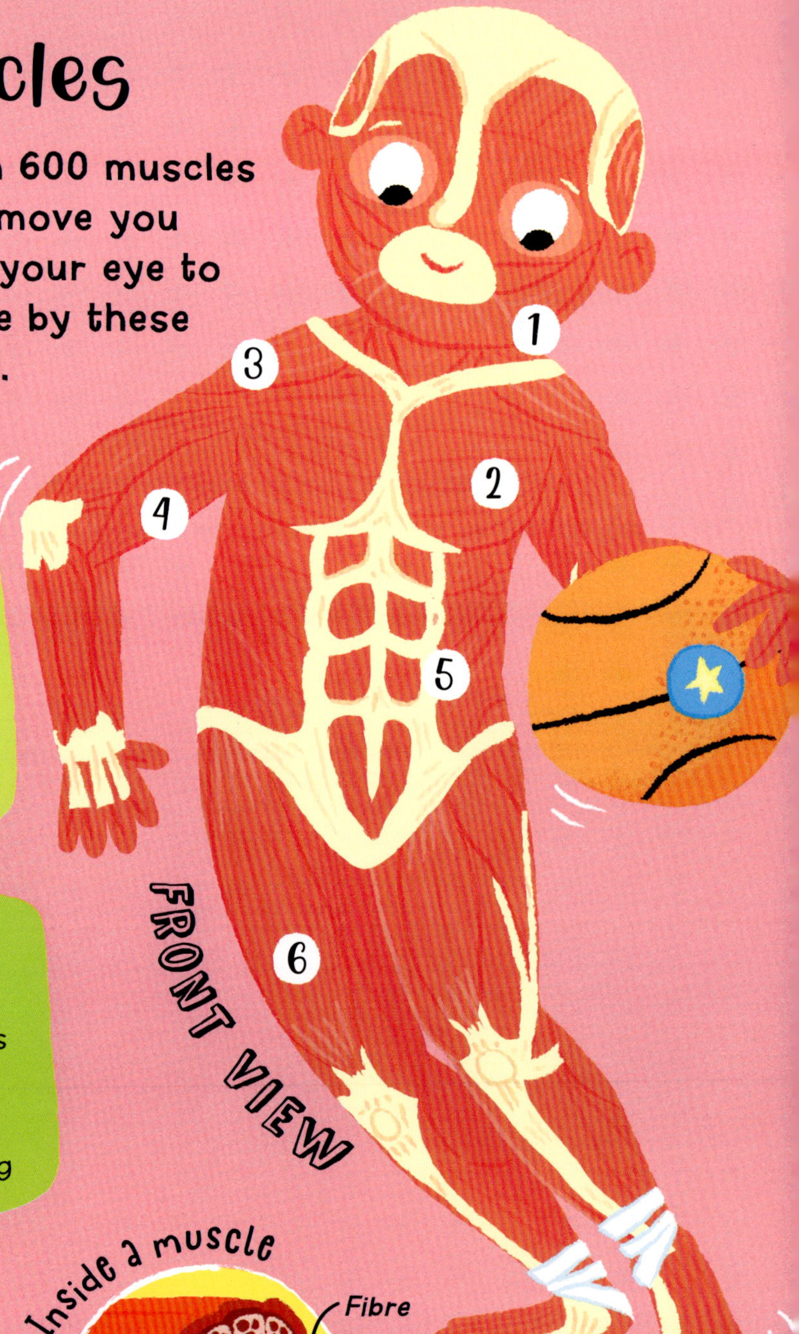

1. Jaw muscles open and close mouth
2. Pectoral muscles move arm and shoulder
3. Deltoid muscles help stretch arm out at the shoulder

4. Biceps muscle bends arm
5. Abdominal muscles help you breathe
6. Thigh muscles straighten your leg

Pulling power

Muscles are made of fibres. Each fibre is made up of long thin cells packed together in bundles.

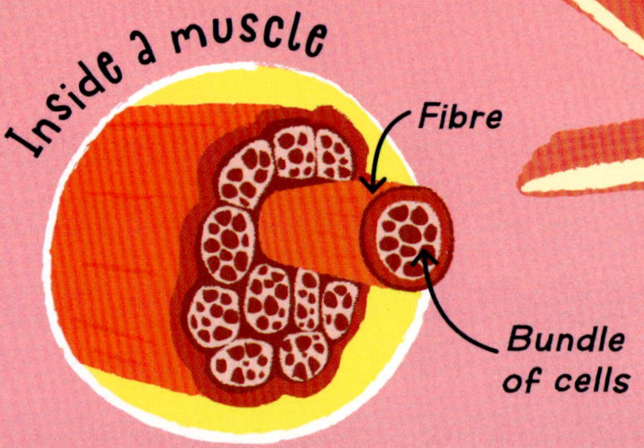

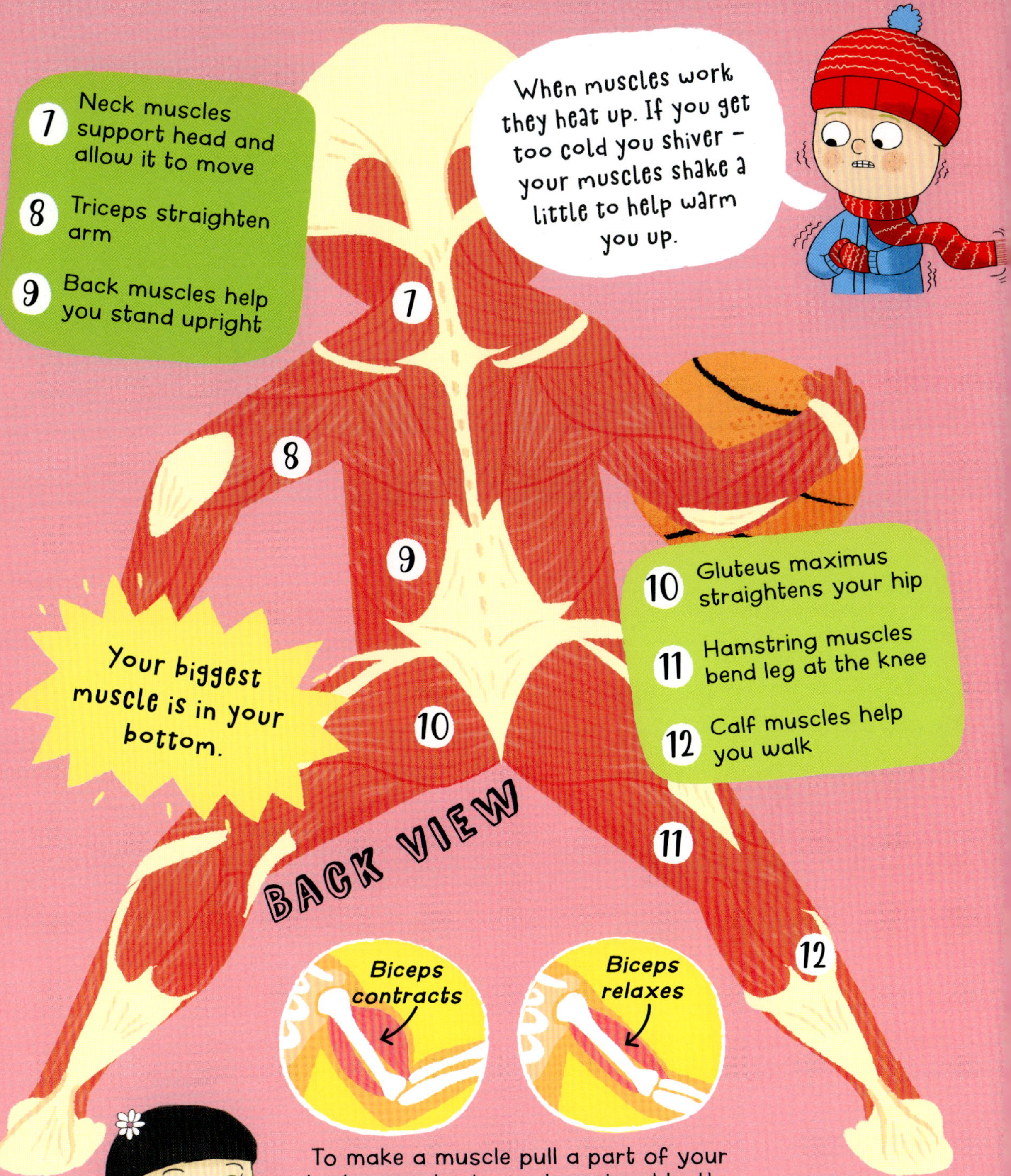

7 Neck muscles support head and allow it to move

8 Triceps straighten arm

9 Back muscles help you stand upright

When muscles work they heat up. If you get too cold you shiver – your muscles shake a little to help warm you up.

10 Gluteus maximus straightens your hip

11 Hamstring muscles bend leg at the knee

12 Calf muscles help you walk

Your biggest muscle is in your bottom.

To make a muscle pull a part of your body, your brain sends a signal to the muscle for its fibres to **contract** (shorten). When the muscle **relaxes**, it returns to its previous length.

On the move

Joints are the places where bones meet. Some joints, like the ones between bones in your skull, are fixed in place. Many other joints allow your body to move in different directions.

Your **elbow** is a **hinge joint**, like the hinge on a door. It can open or close to bend or straighten your arm.

Your **neck** contains a **turning joint**. It allows your head to swivel to the left and right.

Bone home

The bones of moving joints are held in place by strong and stretchy straps called ligaments. Muscles are joined to bones by strong cords called tendons.

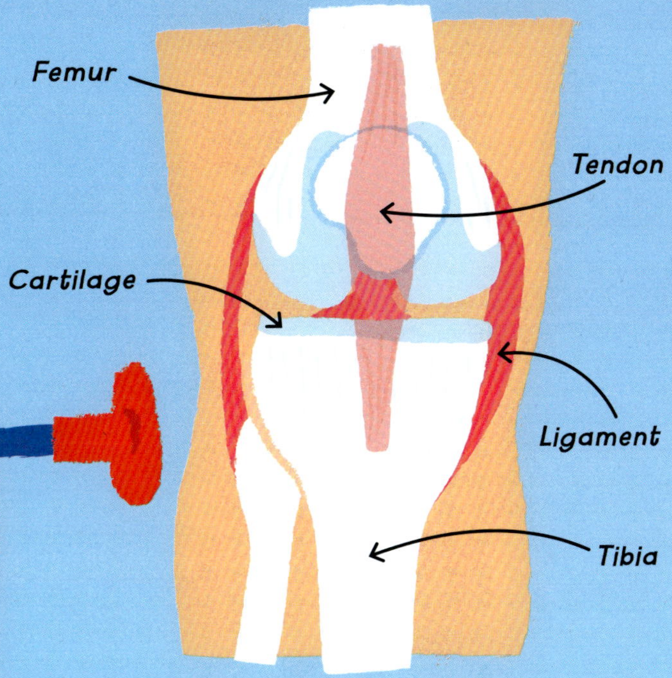

Knee joint

Your **shoulder** is a **ball-and-socket** joint. It can move in a wide range of directions.

A special kind of joint in your foot has bones that slide across each other, which make your feet very flexible.

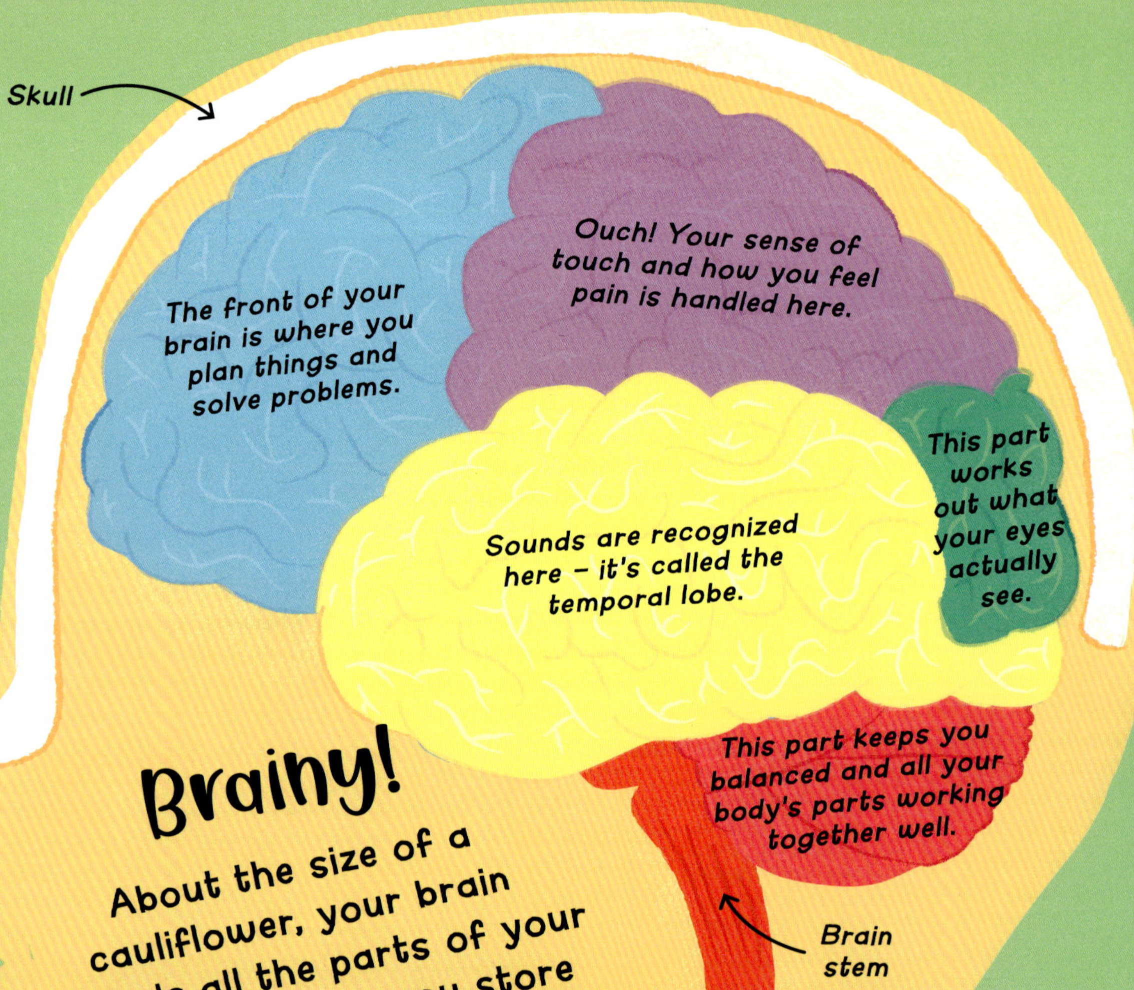

Brainy!

About the size of a cauliflower, your brain controls all the parts of your body. It is where you store memories and have ideas. Different bits of your brain all do different jobs.

Your brain has two sides – left and right. Each half controls the opposite side of your body.

On your nerves

Your body is always chatting to your brain. Its signals travel through the nervous system – a network of nerves that extends all over your body.

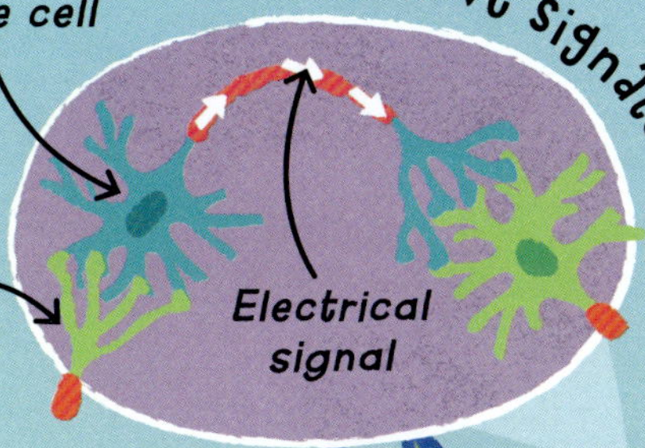

Electric!

Nerves are made up of lots of nerve cells. Signals pass through each nerve cell like tiny sparks of electricity.

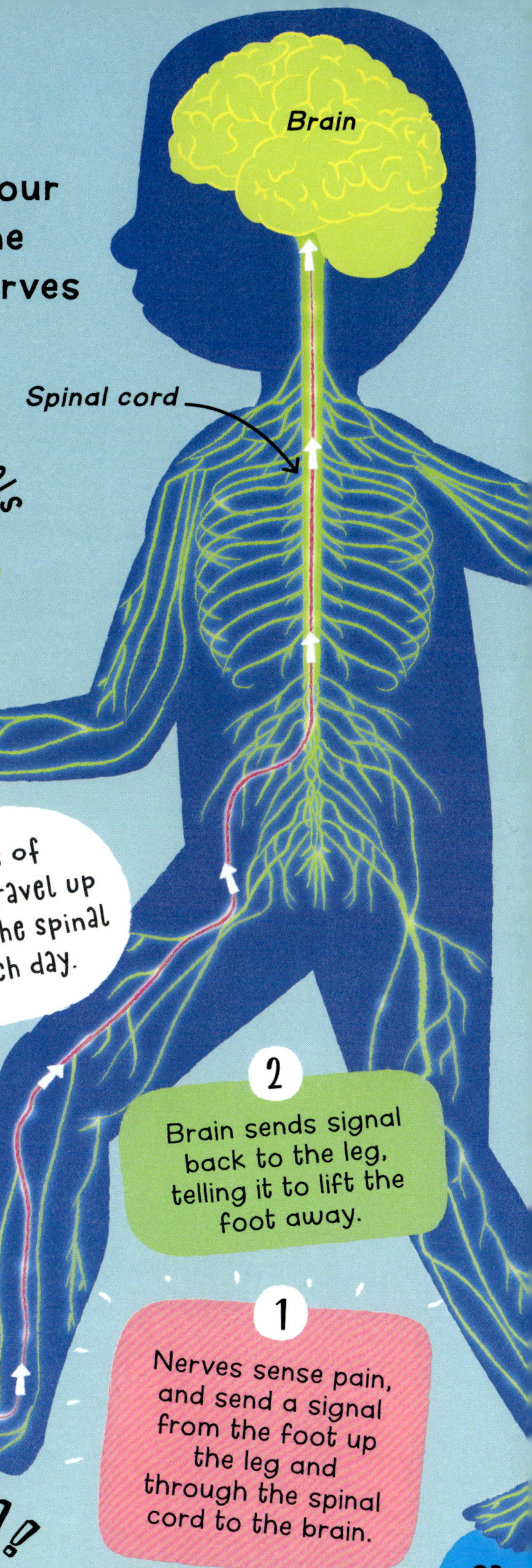

Speedy signals

All parts of your body tell your brain about what is happening and where they are. In return, your brain sends out signals, telling those parts what to do.

Super senses

Your body uses its senses to learn about itself and the world. Senses take in information, turn it into electrical signals, and send it to your brain.

Sight
Your eyes give you your sense of sight. Each eye sees a slightly different view. Your brain puts them together to form a clear picture.

Your sense of balance keeps you upright. Spinning around makes this sense work less well, causing you to feel wobbly and dizzy.

Touch
This sense works all over your body and tells you what objects feel like.

Your skin contains lots of cells that can feel warmth or cold.

Taste
Special cells in your mouth and on your tongue let you taste. Without them, a cookie and a cowpat would taste the same!

Hearing
You can hear a wide range of sounds. Some are high-pitched, like a whistle. Others are low, like the rumble of a thunderstorm.

Smell
Cells inside your nose allow you to recognize thousands of different smells.

Your lips and tongue are the parts of your body most sensitive to heat.

Eye-mazing!

Your eyes let light in. Light travels through your eye to the retina at the back. There, special cells turn light into electrical signals. The signals travel to your brain, which works out what you are seeing.

When you blink, tears wash across your eyeball, cleaning away any grit and dust.

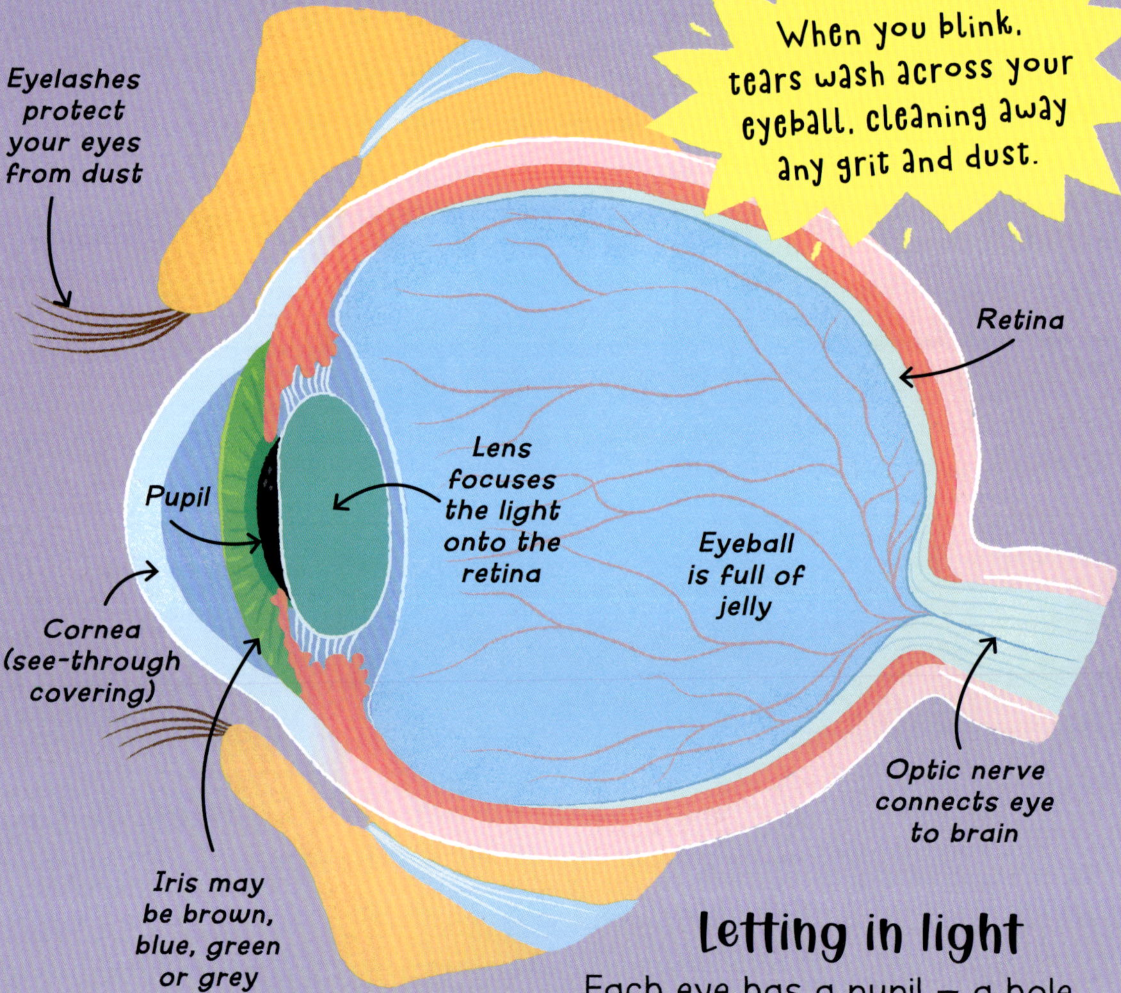

Letting in light

Each eye has a pupil – a hole that lets in light. Around this is an iris containing muscles that change the pupil's size to let in the right amount of light.

All ears

The flaps on the side of your head are just the start of what happens when you hear a sound. Your sense of hearing comes from a chain of events that happens mostly inside your head.

3
The ossicles are three tiny bones. They take vibrations from the eardrum and pass them to the cochlea.

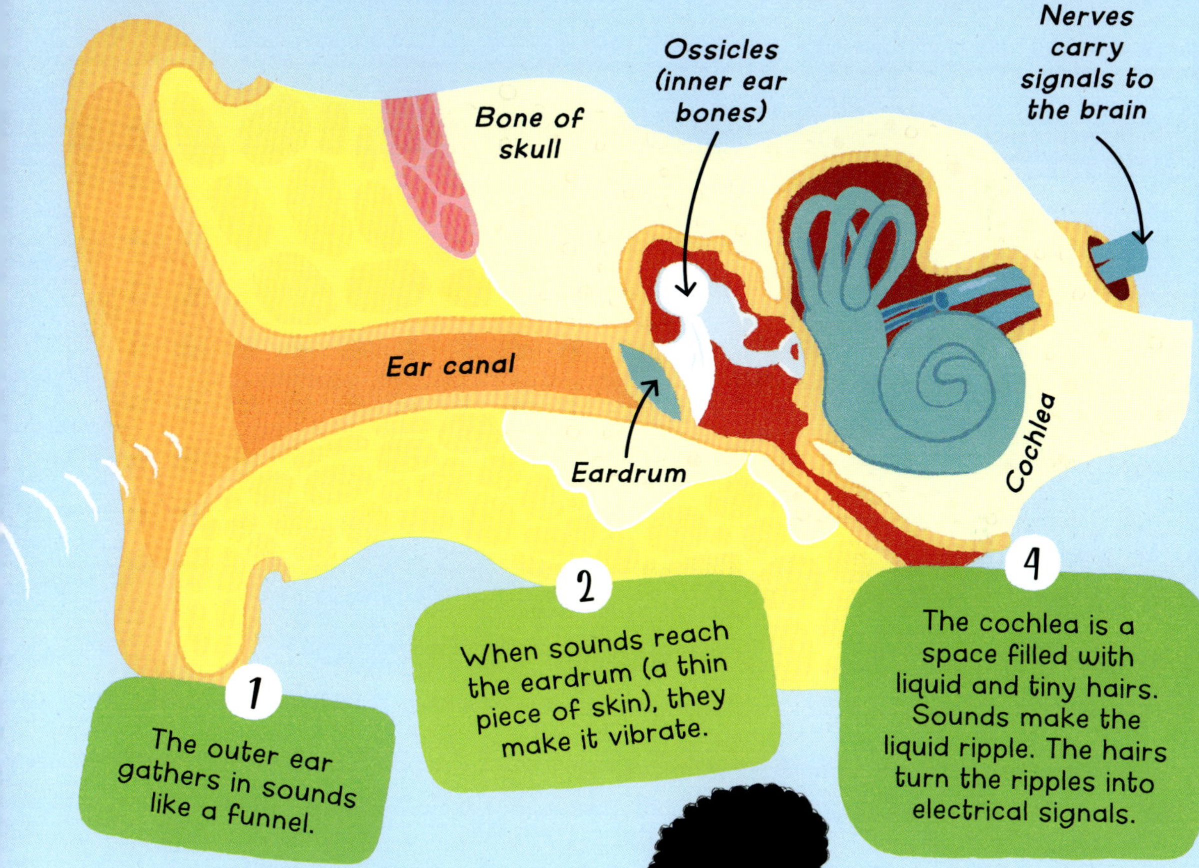

2
When sounds reach the eardrum (a thin piece of skin), they make it vibrate.

4
The cochlea is a space filled with liquid and tiny hairs. Sounds make the liquid ripple. The hairs turn the ripples into electrical signals.

1
The outer ear gathers in sounds like a funnel.

Sounds are **vibrations** in the air. They can be quiet or loud, high or low.

Your beating heart

Your heart is an organ made mostly of muscle. It is one of the most powerful muscles, pumping blood all around the body.

1 Blood low in oxygen enters the right side of your heart.

2 Your heart pumps the low-oxygen blood to your lungs.

Your heart is about the same size as your clenched fist.

Power pump

Your heart is tireless – it beats (pumps) around 100,000 times per day. That's nearly 70 times every minute.

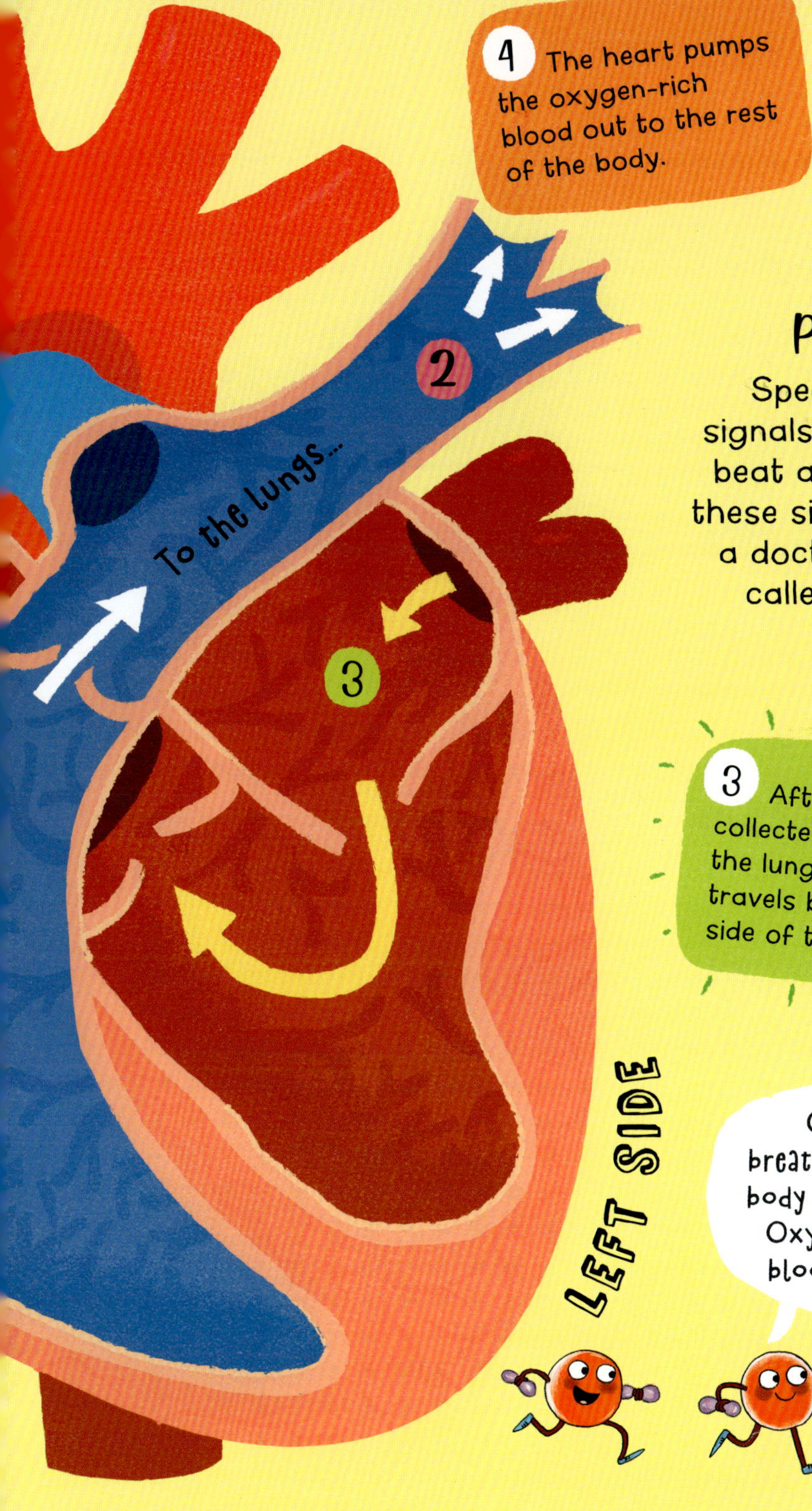

In a year your heart pumps enough blood to fill an Olympic swimming pool!

Pacemakers

Special cells send out signals to make your heart beat at the right speed. If these signals aren't working, a doctor may fit a device called a pacemaker to correct it.

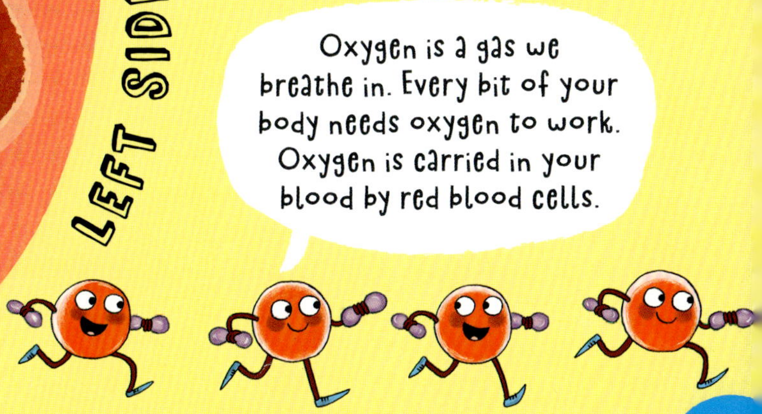

Blood takes a trip

Blood transports useful things around your body such as oxygen and nutrients from food. It's pumped by the strong muscle of your heart. Blood travels through tubes called vessels.

If all your blood vessels were laid end to end, they would go around the world two and a half times!

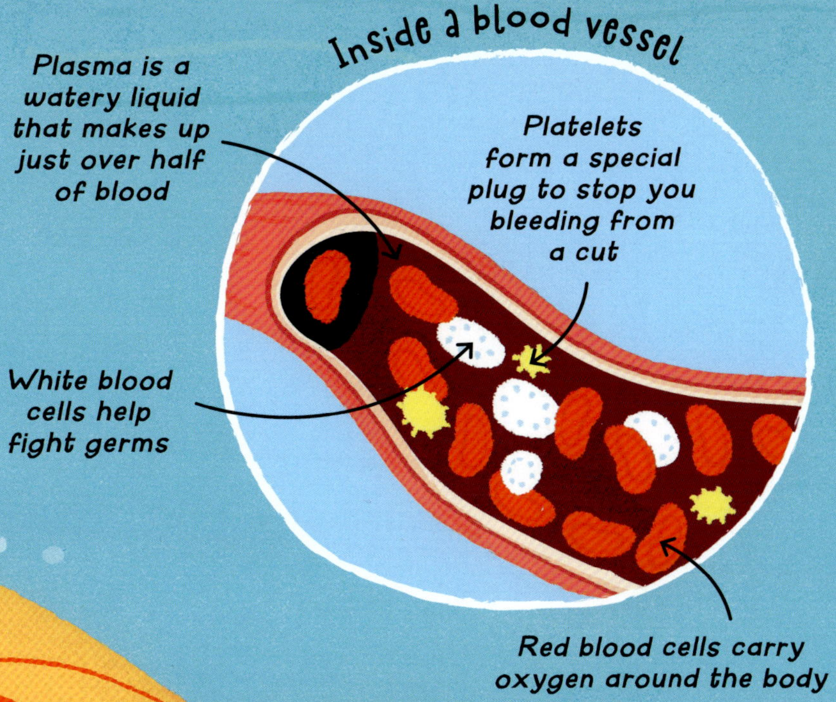

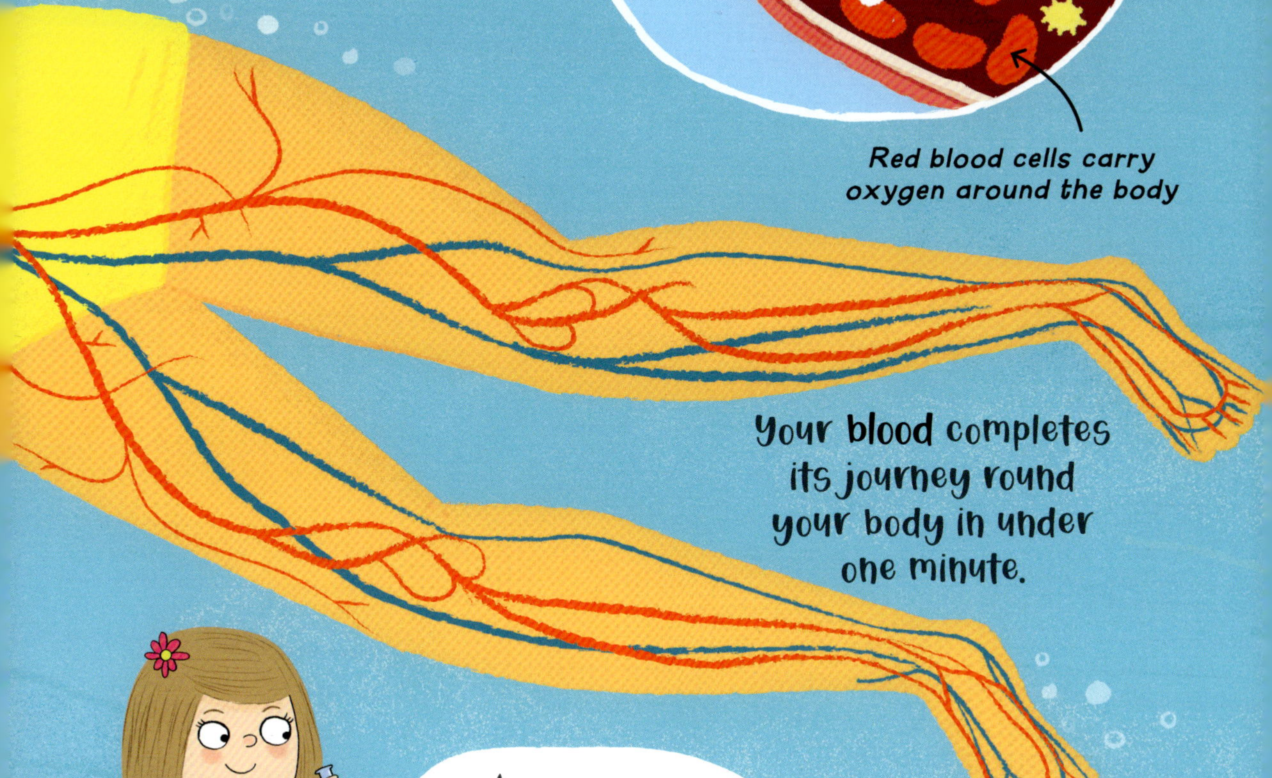

Your blood completes its journey round your body in under one minute.

Breathtaking!

Oxygen is a gas that makes up about one fifth of air. Your body needs lots of oxygen to turn food into energy. You gain oxygen by breathing air into your lungs.

2

Air is sucked into your mouth and nose. It travels down your windpipe, which branches left and right – one branch to each lung.

An average person breathes in more than 8000 litres of air every day.

Your left lung is smaller than your right lung, to make room for your heart.

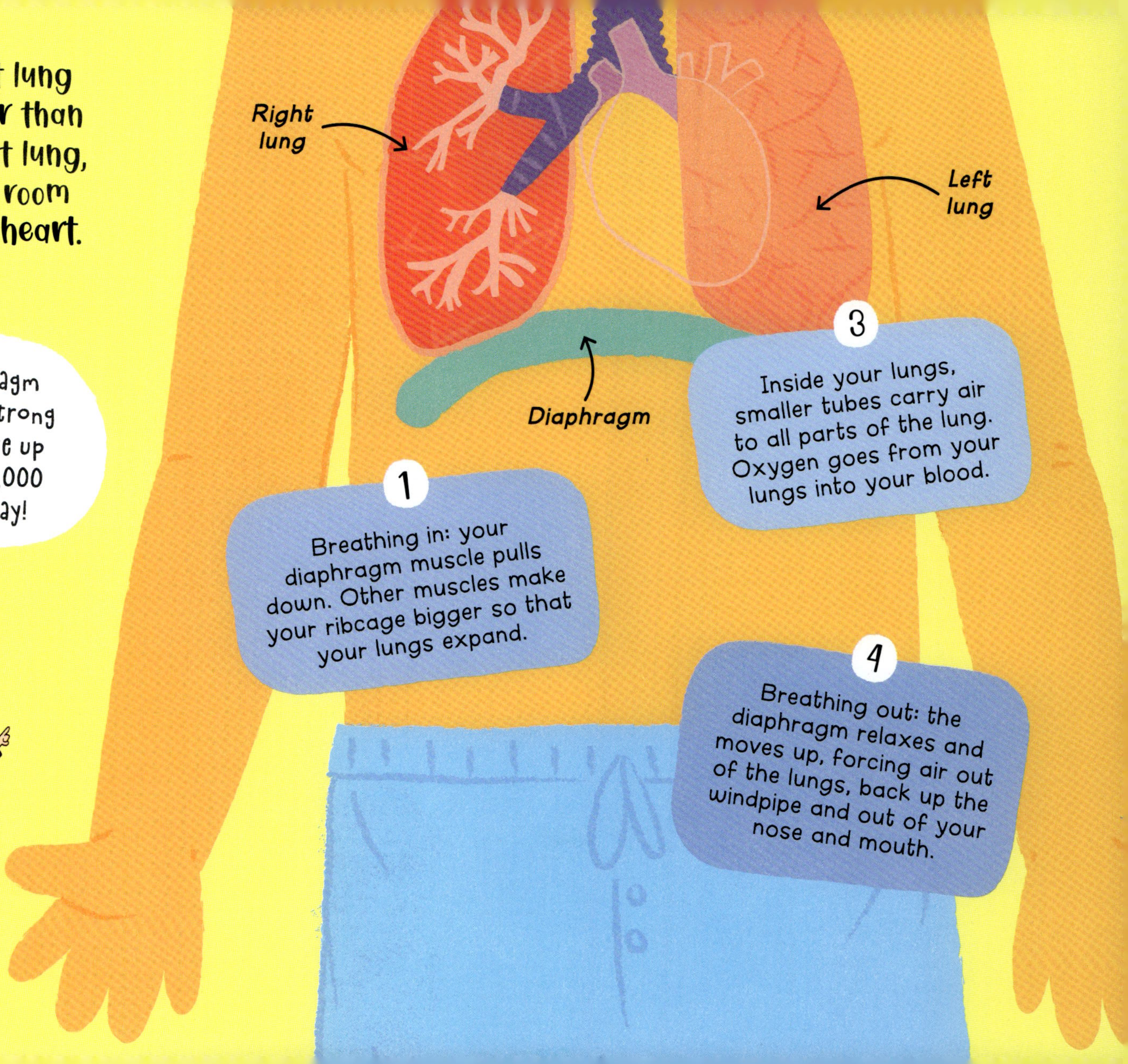

1 Breathing in: your diaphragm muscle pulls down. Other muscles make your ribcage bigger so that your lungs expand.

3 Inside your lungs, smaller tubes carry air to all parts of the lung. Oxygen goes from your lungs into your blood.

4 Breathing out: the diaphragm relaxes and moves up, forcing air out of the lungs, back up the windpipe and out of your nose and mouth.

Open wide!

Your mouth helps you speak, taste and breathe. It is packed full of teeth which cut, grind and chew your food.

Growing up

You'll have two sets of teeth in your life. Your 20 baby teeth start falling out when you're about six years old, and are replaced by a set of 32 adult teeth.

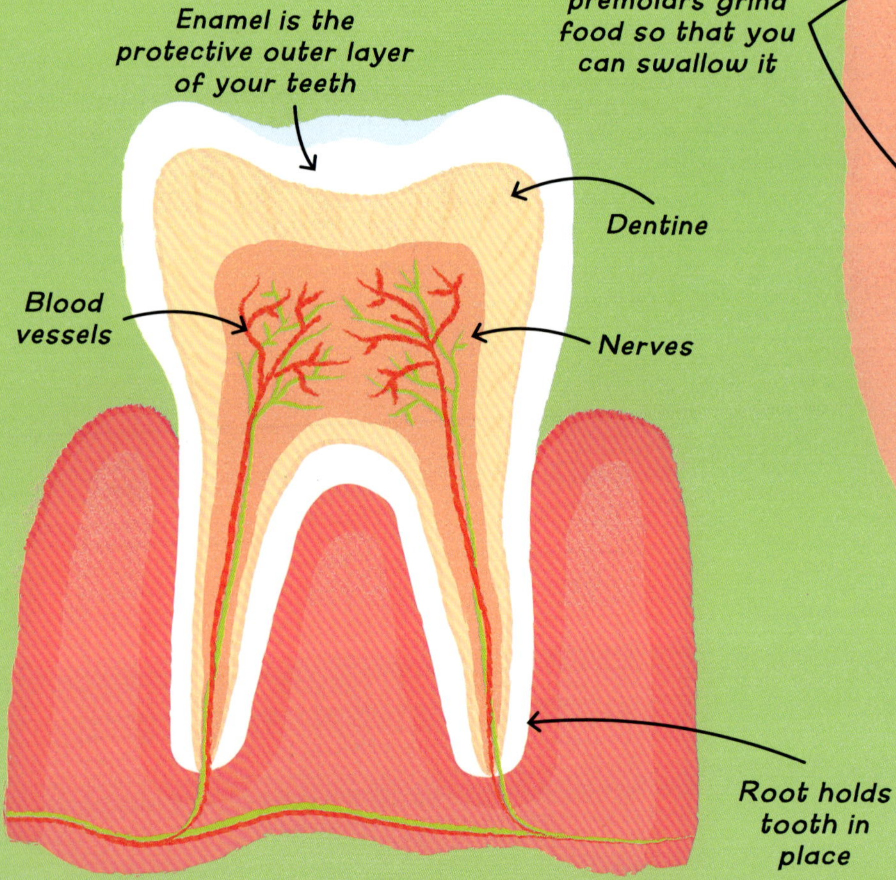

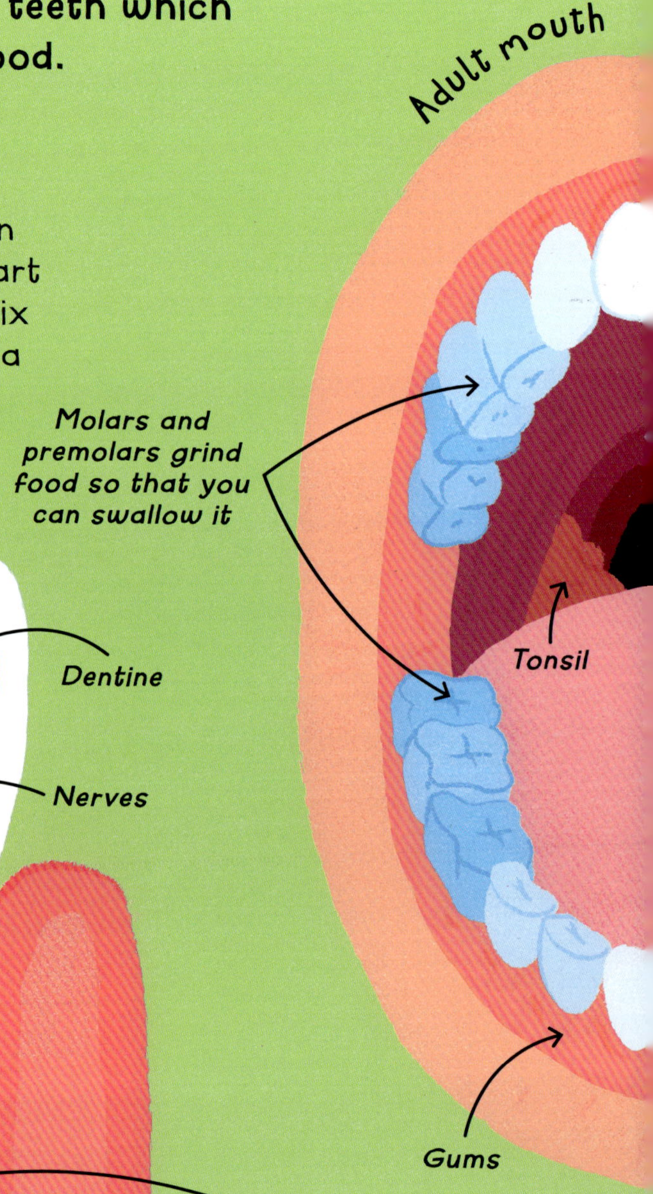

The four canine teeth are more cone-shaped to rip and tear food

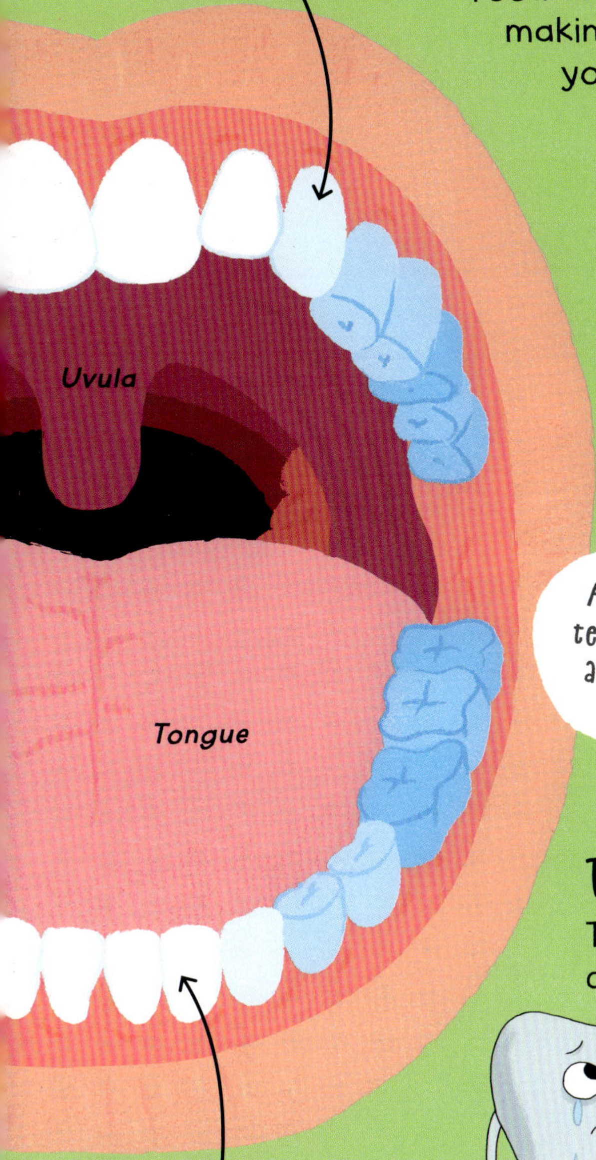

The eight incisor teeth cut and chop food when you bite

Mouth-watering

The liquid in your mouth is called saliva. It helps dissolve some parts of food and wets the rest, making it easier for you to chew.

Enamel is the hardest substance in your whole body.

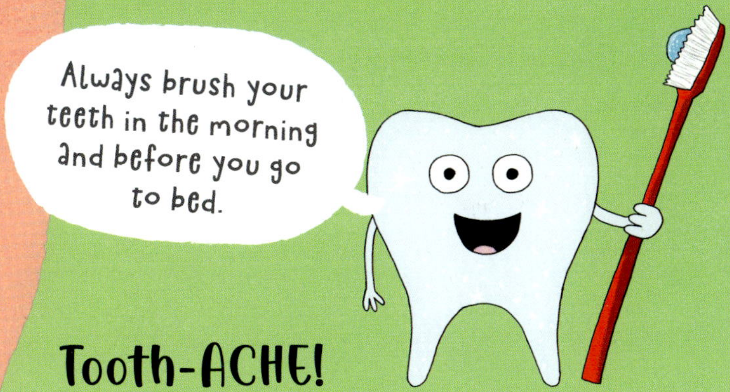

Tooth-ACHE!

The pain of toothache may be caused by the enamel of your teeth being damaged by decay. This can happen if you eat lots of sugary foods and don't brush your teeth well and often.

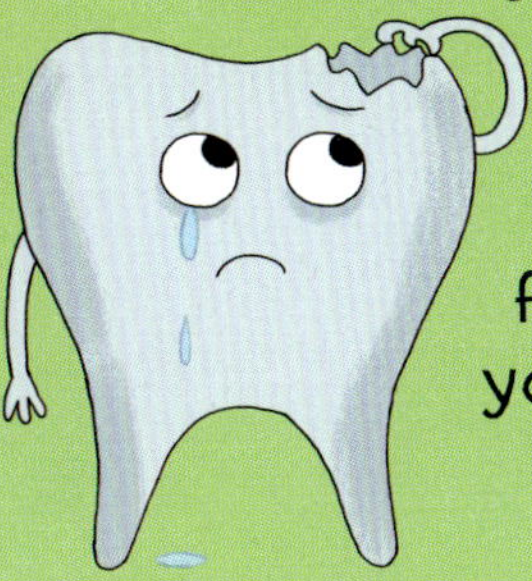

Food's journey

You need food for energy, to stay healthy and for your body to grow and repair itself. When you eat, your food starts a journey through your digestive system.

In your tummy

Your stomach is a stretchy bag which expands to hold a meal. Food is churned around inside it for hours. Strong chemicals turn it into a gloopy soup.

When empty, your stomach is the size of a tennis ball, but when full it can stretch to almost the size of a soccer ball!

Food tube

In the small intestine, food is broken down more. Useful bits go into your blood, to be sent around your body. The rest travels into the large intestine.

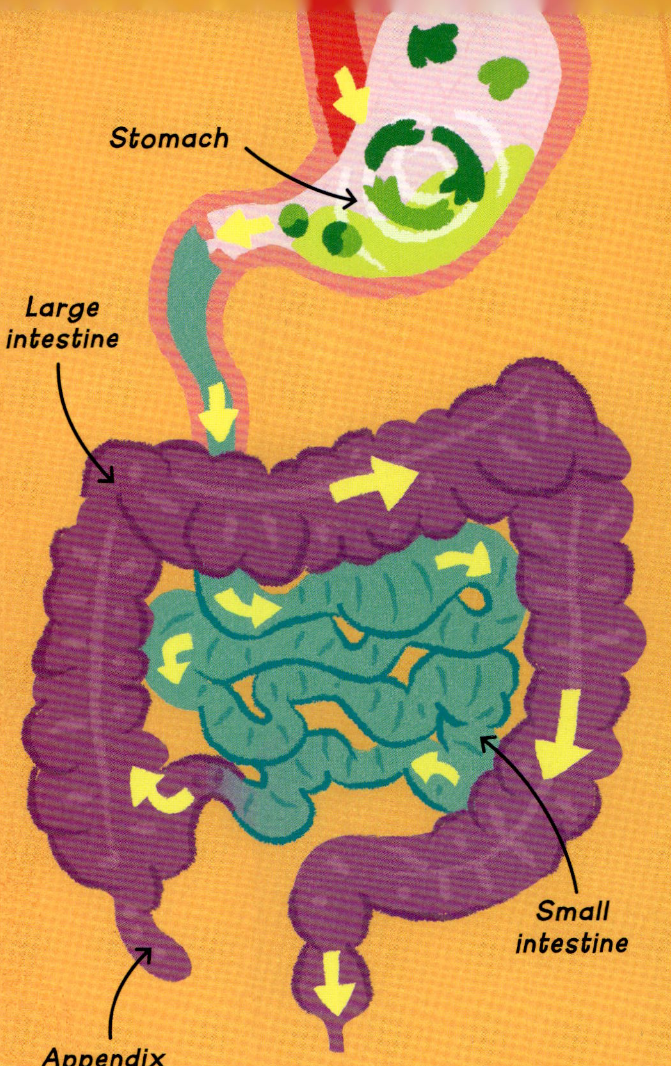

Waste workers

Lots is left behind after all the goodness from your food has travelled into your blood. This waste material sets off on its own journey.

Recycler

The large intestine is about 1.5 metres long. It absorbs water and any last useful bits from food.

Tiny helpers

Millions of bacteria (tiny creatures) live in your large intestine. Many help your body absorb goodness from food. They also create gas which leaves you via your bottom.

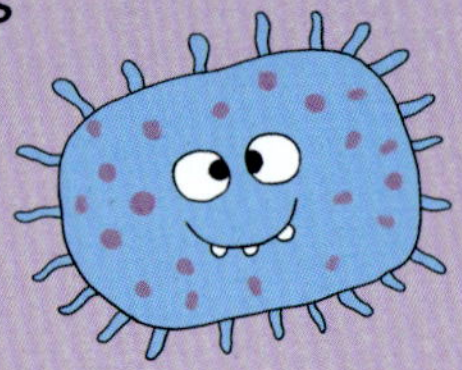

Your poo is about three-quarters **water**. The rest is solid waste. Almost one third of the solid stuff in poo is made up of **dead bacteria!**

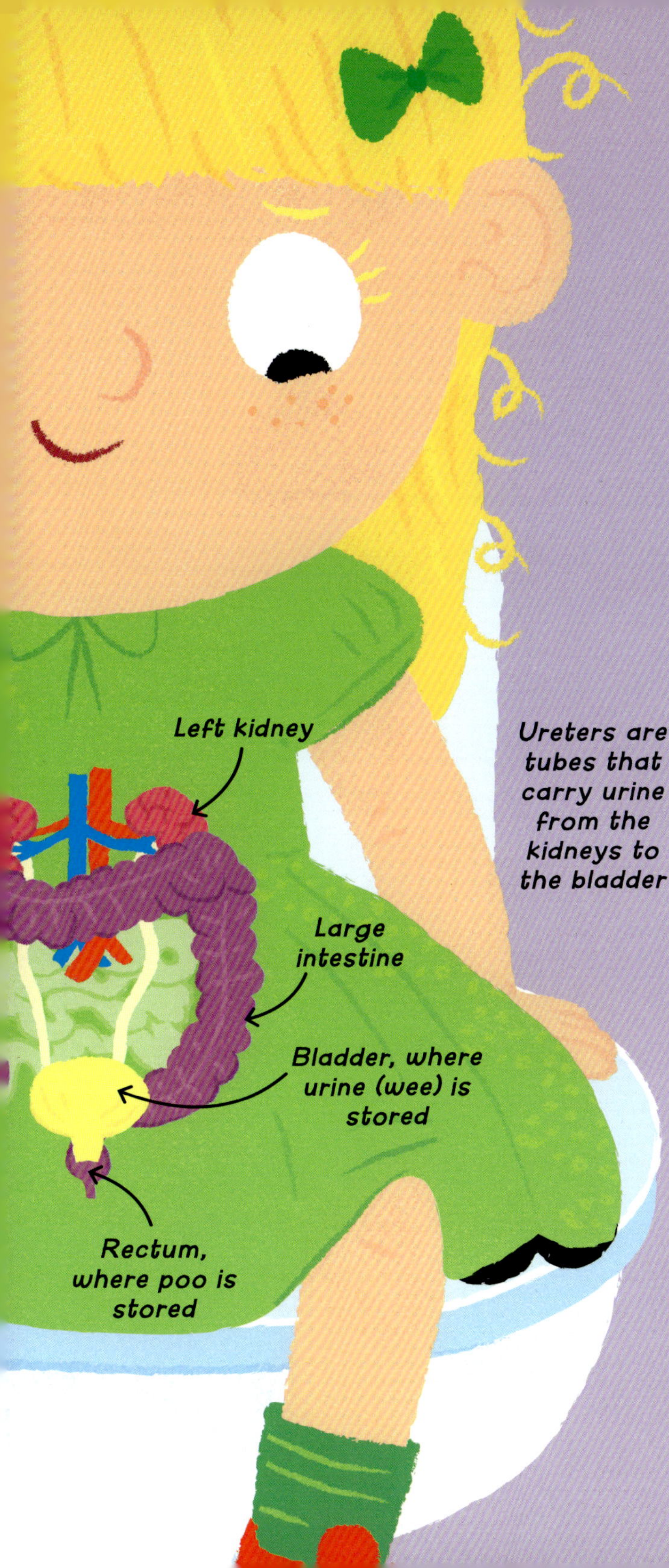

Each kidney gets rid of 1–1.5 litres of urine a day!

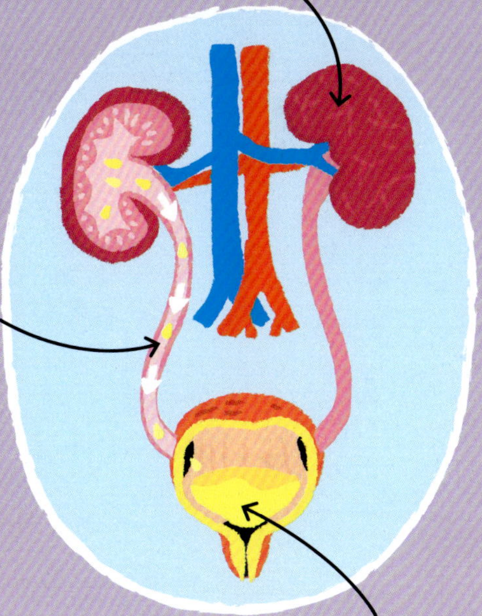

Time to go

Most people's bladders can hold around a third of a litre of urine. When your bladder is full, it sends signals to your brain that it's time to go to the toilet.

Feeling better?

Your amazing body protects you against illness and disease every day. It is also brilliant at repairing itself. Sometimes, though, it needs a little help from doctors and nurses.

Too hot!

A fever is when your body temperature is a lot higher than normal. An adult may use a thermometer to check how hot you are.

Scabby stuff

Blood thickens around a cut or graze on your skin. It then hardens to form a scab which stops germs getting into your body.

More than 200 different viruses can cause you to catch a cold.

Broken bones

Bones are strong but can be broken by an accident such as a fall. Children's bones heal quicker than adults'.

1 Doctors take X-ray photos that let them see inside your body.

2 Plaster cast holds a broken bone in the correct position so that it can heal.

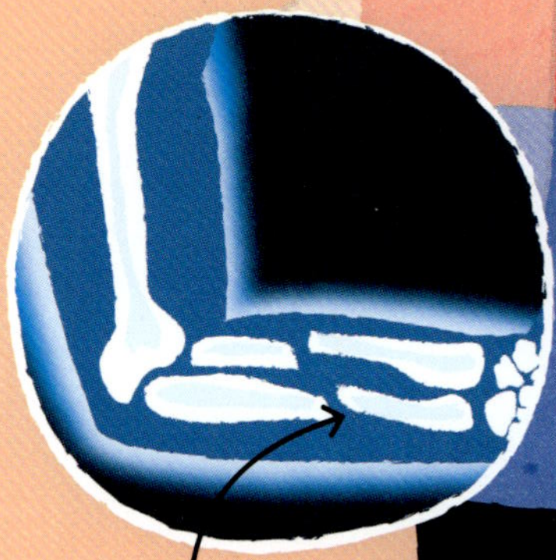

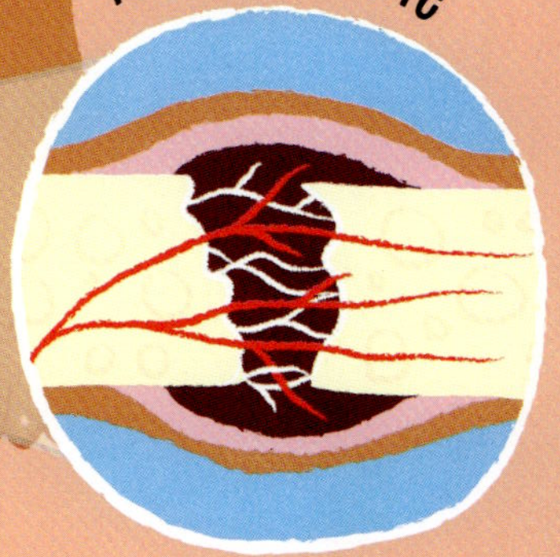

Healing bone

3 Lots of new cells and blood vessels grow where the break occurs. Over time, these repair the bone.

Vaccines helped wipe out a nasty disease called smallpox.

Extra help

A vaccine is made from a weak or harmless version of a disease. It causes your body to build up its defences against the real disease.

RAINFORESTS

It's raining!

It doesn't just rain in a rainforest, it pours! Most rainforests grow in warm places where rain clouds burst open almost every day, drenching everything.

At least 2 **metres** of rain falls every **year** in a rainforest.

Jungle home

A rainforest is a type of habitat, or home. There are lots of places to live and plenty of food to eat.

All the animals and plants in a forest need each other to **survive**. This is called an **ecosystem**.

Jungle life

Forests are full of plants that battle to reach the sunlight. Together, they make a perfect home for a huge variety of animals, from busy ants to hungry elephants.

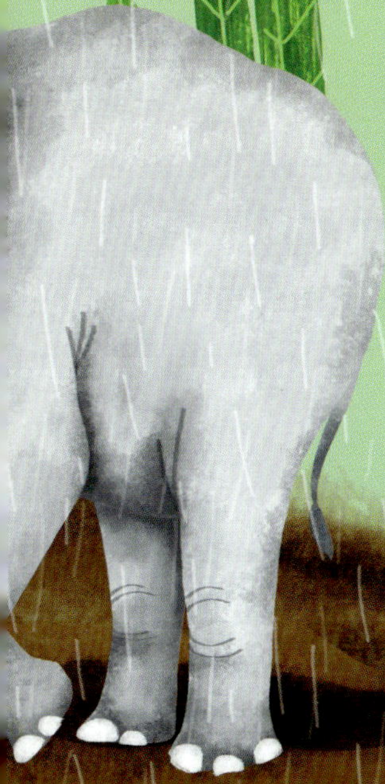

River life

Some of Earth's biggest rivers flow through rainforests. Many animals live in them, and others visit to drink, bathe and cool down.

Caiman (Costa Rica)

Big and scary

Spectacled caimans are members of the crocodile family that can grow to more than 2 metres long. They lay their eggs on the riverbank and guard their nests.

Green anacondas are monster-sized snakes that love swimming.

Pink dolphins

Most dolphins live in the salty sea water, but pink river dolphins live in freshwater instead. River pollution is making it hard for them to survive.

Plants and fungi

Rainforest plants and trees make their own food. They use energy from sunlight to turn water and air into sugars. They return oxygen to the air, help control the weather, and keep the planet cooler.

Hungry fungi

Fungi don't make their own food – so they aren't plants. They live on plants, animals, or rotting things, and take their food in through root-like threads.

Fungi help break down dead plants and animals into the nutrients that plants need to grow.

Lianas are woody plants that hang from tree branches.

Meat-eaters

Pitcher plants eat meat! Bugs fall in and drown in a pool of water inside the jug-shaped trap. The plant then dissolves the bug and eats it.

Titan arum flower stalks can grow more than 3 metres tall. They stink like rotting fish and eggs. Flies love the smell!

In the treetops

Most rainforest animals live in the canopy (top layer), and have developed clever ways to get around.

Flying and leaping

Bats, birds and many bugs fly on wings between trees. Other animals glide, climb or leap instead!

Flying snakes flatten their bodies before a leap. They silently glide through the air, and take their prey by surprise.

Flying lizards stretch out flaps of skin and soar from one branch to another. They can glide 8 metres in one leap!

Jungle birds

Birds love rainforests. There are places to perch, nest and hide. There is plenty of food, too – from small bugs and lizards to seeds, nuts and flowers.

A macaw can measure **one metre** from beak to tail tip!

Satin bowerbird

Making a home

Birds live in all parts of the forest, from the forest floor to the treetops. Tree holes make safe homes for birds that are caring for eggs and chicks.

Southern crowned pigeon

Hyacinth macaws are huge, thanks to their long tail feathers.

Bright and beautiful

A stunning scarlet ibis is easy to spot, even in a dense jungle. Groups of ibises perch on trees near rivers and lakes.

Farmyard chickens are close cousins of plump rainforest birds, called junglefowl.

I beat my wings in a figure-of-eight shape so I can hover at a flower and sip the nectar.

Showing off

Male birds of paradise are glamorous! They dance, sing and show off their fine feathers.

Monkeys and apes

Like us, monkeys and apes belong to a group of animals called primates. They are clever, furry animals with hands. Primates live in family groups, and parents teach their babies how to find food.

Stick-tastic!

Chimpanzees are our closest relatives. They poke sticks into termite nests to get food.

Gibbons hoot and holler at each other across the treetops.

HOOT!

HOWL!

Gibbon

Howler monkeys are the loudest primates. They can be heard from far away.

Apes don't have tails, unlike most monkeys.

Mountain gorillas

It can get chilly in the African cloud forest. The trees drip, and damp fog hangs in the air, so mountain gorillas need extra-thick fur.

On the prowl

Beware – these predators are silent and deadly! Cats have super senses to see, smell and hear small animals scuttling in the shadows.

Helpful hairs

Whiskers help a cat to feel its way in the dark and work out the size of obstacles in its path. Whiskers are so sensitive they can even detect changes in the air.

Acrobat cats

Clouded leopards are fast, springy and superb climbers. They spend most of their lives in the canopy, sleeping or chasing monkeys.

Snakes and lizards

Reptiles are scaly-skinned animals that bask in the sun to warm up. Most lay eggs. Snakes and lizards are reptiles, and lots of them live in rainforests.

Tongue-tastic!

There are more than 70 types of chameleon on the island of Madagascar. These lizards are often brightly coloured and catch bugs with a long, sticky tongue!

Gaboon vipers are camouflaged for life on the forest floor. These snakes have fangs that they use to inject deadly venom.

Snakes and lizards move easily between the canopy and the understorey.

Listen for the sound of a tokay gecko calling out for mates.

Coral snakes and **milk snakes** look similar, but only coral snakes are venomous. Could you tell the difference if you saw one in a jungle?

The forest floor

In a rainforest there is a whole world at your feet to explore. Many animals live in this special habitat, including those you can't easily see.

Fungi often have strange names, such as wood ear, pink disco and turkey tail.

Hiding places

It's dark and damp down here, but there are plenty of things to eat and places to hide. Some animals live beneath trees or in underground burrows.

Long-beaked echidnas are unusual mammals because they lay eggs.

Inside their large nests, **termites** munch up wood and make a mixture with their poo where fungi grow. The termites eat the fungi.

Leaf litter lunch

Small mammals such as tenrecs and shrews look for worms and grubs on the ground.

Sengis are also called elephant shrews, because their long, bendy snouts look like trunks.

Bugs and spiders

Insects do one of the animal kingdom's most important jobs: they pollinate flowers when they feed on them. This means that the flowers can grow seeds, which will one day grow into new plants.

Birdwing butterfly

Birdwing butterflies are the world's largest, with a wingspan of 20 centimetres or more.

Fungus farming

Leafcutter ants cut up pieces of leaf, carry them back to their nest, and use them to feed their fungus garden. The ants eat the fungus that grows there and feed it to their babies, too.

Sabre-wing butterflies whizz around above the tall trees, visiting flowers.

Praying mantises wait for other bugs to pass by, then attack, holding the victim tight with spiky limbs.

Orb-web spiders spin silk between trees to build sticky webs, some as large as a person!

Orchid bees are brightly coloured in metallic reds, greens and blues. They collect nectar and pollen from orchid flowers.

Giant spiders

Tarantulas hunt other bugs, but some are big enough to catch frogs and birds. They kill their victim with a bite and then suck out its insides, like soup!

OCEANS

What are oceans?

Oceans are very big areas of salty water. Most of the water in our world is in the oceans. They are so vast and deep that we have only explored a tiny part of them.

Water for life

The oceans are full of life. We know lots about life near the surface, but there are huge numbers of mysterious creatures lurking in the depths.

Life on Earth probably started in the oceans billions of years ago.

As much as 80 percent of all living things on Earth live in the oceans.

Rivers wash salt off the land into the sea, making it salty.

Deep-sea vampire squid use their sticky suckers to collect dead animals and poop – yuck!

World of water

The three biggest oceans are the Pacific, the Atlantic and the Indian Oceans. Two smaller and colder oceans are the Arctic and Southern Oceans. Together they make one huge world ocean.

The **Atlantic Ocean** is the second biggest ocean, but it is only about half the size of the **Pacific**.

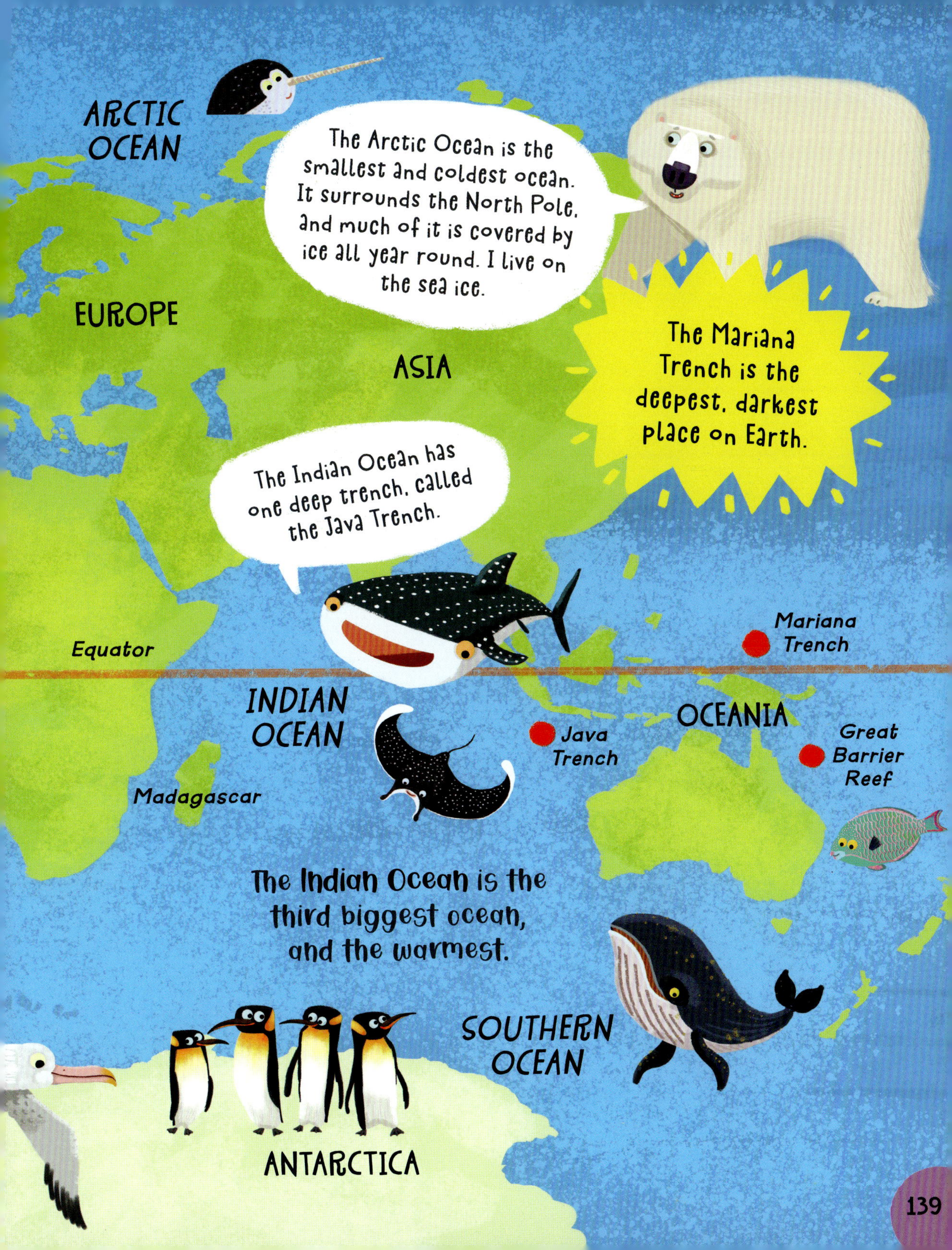
ARCTIC OCEAN
The Arctic Ocean is the smallest and coldest ocean. It surrounds the North Pole, and much of it is covered by ice all year round. I live on the sea ice.
EUROPE
ASIA
The Mariana Trench is the deepest, darkest place on Earth.
The Indian Ocean has one deep trench, called the Java Trench.
Equator
Mariana Trench
INDIAN OCEAN
OCEANIA
Java Trench
Great Barrier Reef
Madagascar
The Indian Ocean is the third biggest ocean, and the warmest.
SOUTHERN OCEAN
ANTARCTICA

Oceans on the move

Water is always moving, both on the surface and in the depths. The wind moves water on the surface, while deep water movement depends on how hot, cold or salty the water is.

Waves

As the wind blows over the oceans, it makes ripples, or waves, on the surface. The size of a wave depends on the strength of the wind and how long it has been blowing.

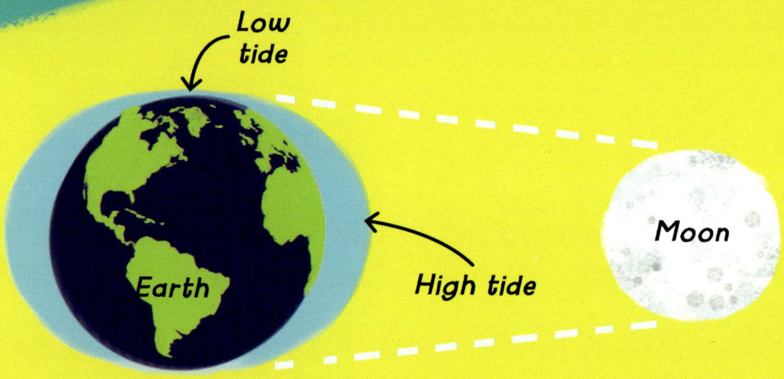

Tides

On most shorelines, the water moves up and down the beach twice a day. These movements are called tides. Tides happen when the Moon pulls on the water in the oceans.

Life at the top

In the open ocean, most plants and animals live near the sunny surface waters. Billions of tiny drifting plants and animals, called plankton, provide food for larger animals, from fish and turtles to seals and whales.

Food chains

Living things in the ocean are linked together into food chains. Most food chains start with plant plankton, which float in the water and make their own food using the Sun's energy.

Why is the sea blue?

Sunlight is made up of all the rainbow colours, but the sea 'swallows' the red colours. Blue light scatters and is reflected back into our eyes, making the sea look blue.

Blue and green light go deeper down in the sea than the other colours

Shallow waters

A rich variety of plants and animals live in underwater meadows and seaweed forests near the shore. Mangrove trees also create flooded forests full of life on sheltered shorelines.

Sea otters visit kelp forests to hunt for sea urchins, which eat the leaf-like kelp fronds.

Kelp forests

A giant seaweed called kelp forms thick, underwater forests near the shores of many cool oceans.

Mangrove forests

Along warm shorelines, trees called mangroves survive in the salty, muddy water. The mud does not contain much oxygen for breathing, so the trees grow special breathing roots.

Seagrass meadows

Seagrasses are the only flowering plants that live in the oceans. They grow mainly on sunny sea floors in warm water.

Rock pools

When the tide goes out on the beach, little pools of water are left behind among the rocks. Some plants and animals make their homes in these rock pools.

Out of the water, sea anemones pull in their tentacles. They look like blobs of jelly

Shelly armour

Animals such as limpets and barnacles cling tightly to the rocks. Their tough shells protect them from waves and predators, and also stop them drying out.

Water wings

Bladder wrack seaweed has little 'water wings' full of air. They help it to float on the surface of the water when the tide comes in. It can trap the sunlight it needs to make food.

A starfish can let go of one of its arms to escape a predator. A new arm grows to replace the old one!

Blennies have slimy skin that helps them slide between rocks, where they like to hide.

Down in the deep

In the deep ocean, the water is inky black, and very cold and heavy. There is not enough light for plants to survive. Animals feed on each other, or dead animals that sink down from the surface.

The giant squid has the biggest eyes of any animal. Each eye is bigger than a football!

Glow-in-the-dark

A lot of deep-sea animals use ghostly glowing lights to flash messages to each other in the darkness.

Lanternfish
Bacteria living inside us make food that we can eat!
I have a huge mouth so I can eat mega meals when I find food.
Gulper eel
Giant tube worms like us live around rocky underwater chimneys. These are formed by minerals spewed out of cracks in the deep ocean floor!

Islands

Dotted all over the oceans are pieces of land surrounded by water called islands. The wind, water and birds carry plants to islands, while animals may fly, swim or drift there.

Island giants

With few predators and less competition for food, some island animals grow into giants. A giant tortoise from the Galapagos Islands may be as heavy as three men.

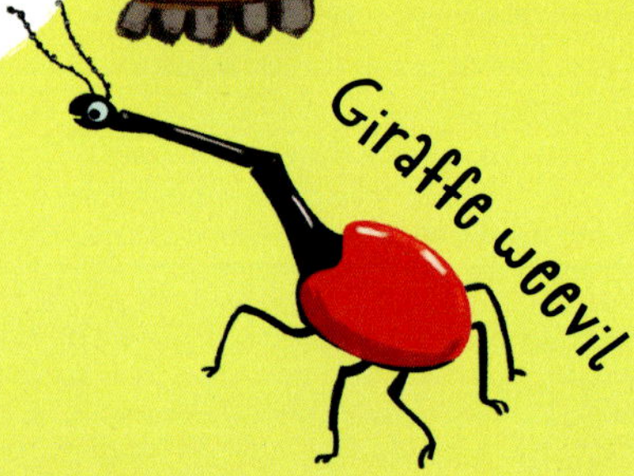

Where islands come from

Islands form when land is cut off from the mainland by the sea (1), and when volcanoes (2) or coral reefs (3) build up new areas of land above the ocean waves.

1. Sea floods land

2. Underwater volcano

3. Coral reefs

Coral reefs

Many coral reefs grow in warm, shallow ocean waters. They are made of millions of hard skeletons of dead animals, called corals. Living corals perch on top of the dead ones.

Corals come in many different shapes. They may look like a deer's antlers, tables, fingers, mushrooms or even brains!

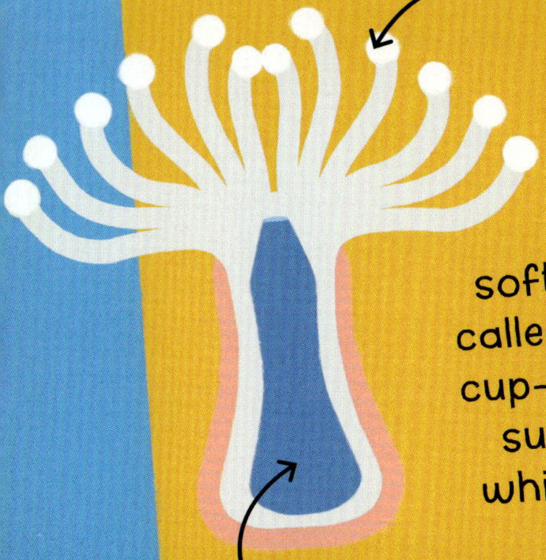

Inside a coral

A stony coral is a small animal with a soft, tube-shaped body called a polyp. It makes a cup-like outer skeleton to support its soft body, which is mainly a mouth and big stomach.

Now you see me...

The bright colours of some ocean animals are a warning message to predators. They say, 'Leave me alone or I will hurt you!'

When the Atolla jellyfish is threatened by a predator, it gives off flashes of blue light to attract more predators, which chase away the first.

Stealing stings

Some sea slugs steal stinging cells from other ocean creatures, such as jellyfish or sea anemones. They store these stings in the tips of finger-like tentacles.

Danger rings

The blue rings on a blue-ringed octopus tell you that it is poisonous. The rings get brighter if the octopus is disturbed.

...now you don't

The Sargasso Sea is an area of warm, calm water. Huge mats of golden sargassum seaweed float in the water and are full of hidden animals.

The **shrimp** looks like the air-filled floats of the sargassum seaweed.

The **frogfish** uses its front fins like arms to climb through the seaweed.

Being invisible

The camouflage colours and patterns of some sargassum seaweed animals help them to hide from predators.

Crab

Tiny **pygmy seahorses** look just like pieces of coral.

Ocean fish

Fish have lived at all levels in the oceans for millions of years. They breathe underwater and use their fins for swimming.

The Atlantic bluefin tuna may weigh more than a horse!

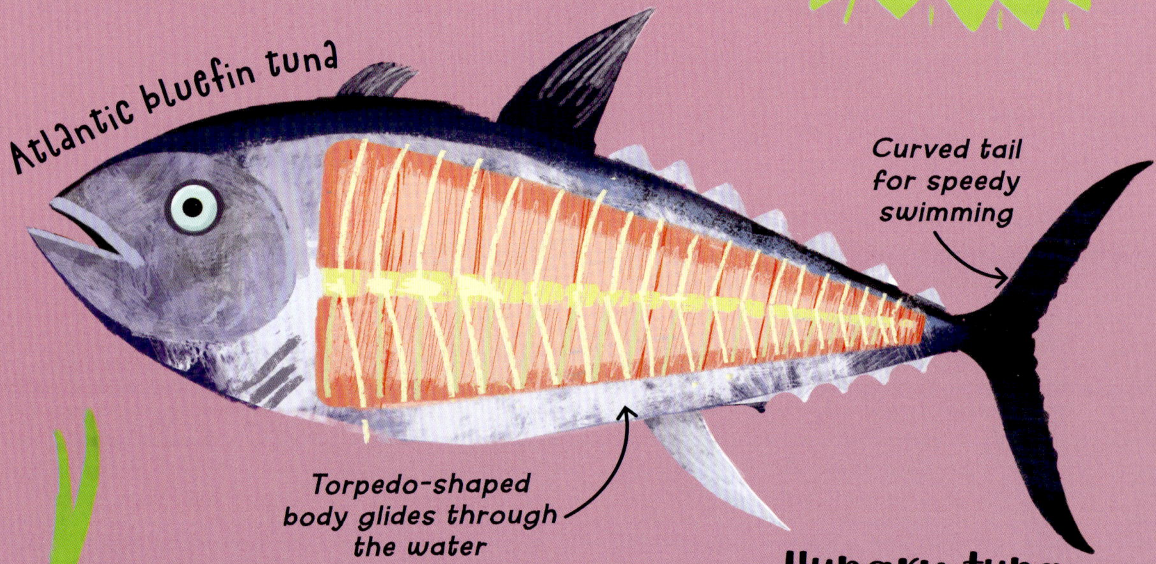

Hungry tuna

Tuna are one of the top predators in the open ocean. These super-fish have a huge appetite and speed through the water chasing smaller fish.

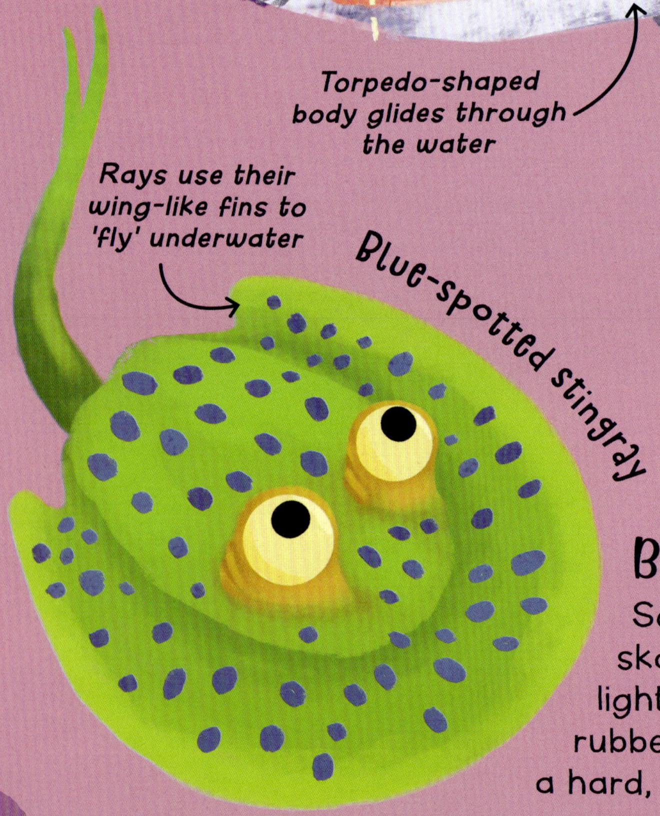

Bendy body

Some fish, such as rays, skates and sharks, have a light, bendy skeleton made of rubbery cartilage. Most fish have a hard, bony skeleton.

Sharks

Over 500 different types of shark swim through the world's oceans. The smallest sharks fit onto a person's hand, but the biggest are as heavy as a bus!

Some sharks lay eggs, but others give birth to baby sharks, called pups.

Mega mouth

The whale shark is the biggest fish in the oceans, but its food is tiny! Whale sharks use bristles on their gills to trap microscopic plankton from the seawater.

Hammer for a head

The acrobatic great hammerhead shark turns its wide head from side to side to sense its surroundings, catch prey, find its way and save energy while swimming.

Flipper feet

Seals, sea lions and walruses have flippers instead of feet, and are agile, playful and speedy swimmers. They dive underwater to catch food, but rest and give birth on beaches or floating sea ice.

A walrus can eat up to 4000 clams in one meal!

A harp seal pup has a fluffy white coat to keep warm and hide from predators on the white ice

Growing up

Baby seals, sea lions and walruses drink their mother's rich milk, which is full of energy.

What big teeth you have!

Walruses use their big teeth, called tusks, for cutting breathing holes in the ice, and for pulling their heavy bodies out of the water onto floating sea ice. Males also use their tusks to fight with rivals.

Ocean reptiles

In dinosaur times, lots of scaly reptiles swam through the world's oceans. Today, only a few ocean reptiles survive. Most of them live close to the shore in warm waters.

When the baby turtles hatch out, they race down to the sea and swim away as fast as they can

Eggs and babies

Most ocean reptiles have to come onto land to lay their eggs. Female sea turtles use their flippers to dig nesting holes on sandy beaches. Then they lay their eggs in the warm sand.

Deadly bite

Sea snakes have a poisonous bite. This helps them to kill prey, such as fish, quickly, before it has a chance to swim away.

Seabirds

Hundreds of birds catch food in the oceans, but lay their eggs and raise their chicks on cliffs or on the seashore. Seabirds have waterproof feathers and webbed feet.

Super wings

The wandering albatross has the longest wings of any bird, measuring more than 3 metres from one wingtip to the other.

Fabulous fisher folk

Albatrosses and gulls feed from the surface, while gannets and brown pelicans dive deep down. Puffins and cormorants swim underwater to catch their prey.

Index